WOMEN WHO KEPT THE LIGHTS

AN ILLUSTRATED HISTORY OF FEMALE LIGHTHOUSE KEEPERS

SECOND EDITION

Sidebar 10. Annie Bell Hobbs at Boon Island Light Station,
Maine, 1876 144

XVIII. Mary Smith at Ediz Hook Light Station,
Washington, 1870-1874, and Point Fermin Light
Station, 1874-1882; Thelma Austin at Point Fermin
Light Station, California, 1925-1941 147

XIX. Kate McDougal at Mare Island Light Station,
California, 1881-1916 151

XX. Laura Hecox at Santa Cruz Light Station, California,
1883-1917 161

XXI. Kate Walker at Robbins Reef Light Station, New
York, 1894-1919 167

XXII. Ellen Wilson at Port Pontchartrain Light Station,
Louisiana, 1882-1896; Margaret Norvell at Head of
Passes Light Station, 1891-1896, Port Pontchartrain
Light Station, 1896-1924, and New Canal Light
Station, Louisiana, 1924-1932 177

Sidebar 11. Other Nineteenth-Century Women Keepers 180

XXIII. Emma Tabberrah at Cumberland Head Light
Station, New York, 1904-1919 189

XXIV. Fannie Salter at Turkey Point Light Station,
Maryland, 1925-1947 193

XXV. The U.S. Coast Guard Runs the Lighthouse Service 201

Epilogue 203

Appendix: Women Who Kept the Lights, 1776-1947 209

Bibliography 225

Index 229

About the Authors 241

The first lighthouse in the American colonies, Boston Harbor Light Station was built on Little Brewster Island in Boston Harbor in 1716. A tax on all vessels using the harbor paid for maintaining the light. Boston Light Station was one of 12 colonial lighthouses that came under federal ownership after the War for Independence, and is the only lighthouse in the United States that still has an official U.S. Coast Guard keeper on site today. Courtesy of the National Archives, #26-LG-5-55.

I. INTRODUCTION

The first woman known to keep a lighthouse in America—Hannah Thomas—owned property with her husband on a long narrow spit of land that forms the protective northern arm around Plymouth Harbor. Local records tell us that the lighthouse with its twin lanterns was built in 1768 on land belonging to John Thomas. Massachusetts Bay Colony paid him rent of five shillings for his land and £200 a year to act as keeper. In 1776 John Thomas joined a Massachusetts regiment and went off to fight the British, leaving Hannah in charge of the lights on Gurnet Point.

Very little is known of Hannah Thomas's experiences through the long years of the War for Independence. Hostile British frigates cruised up and down the coast. The lights were extinguished to keep them from aiding the enemy, but the property was attacked and a garrison stationed there to protect it. When the war ended, widowed Hannah hired a man to help her tend the lights.

When the colonies formed the United States, Gurnet Point was one of the 12 existing lighthouses that came under federal ownership and became the responsibility of the Treasury Department.

In 1792 Alexander Hamilton, Secretary of the Treasury, wrote to Tench Coxe, Commissioner of the Revenue, as follows:[1]

> Pursuant to the 6th Section of the act making alterations in the Treasury and War Departments, I have concluded to commit to you the general superintendence of the Light Houses and other establishments relating to the security of navigation, according to the powers invested in me by law. Information will be given accordingly to the respective Superintendents, who will be instructed to correspond in future with you and take your directions.

When the President's sanction is in any case required, you will make report to me, in order that the requisite submission to him may be made.

Local customs collectors were appointed superintendents of lighthouses for their regions. Fourteen more light stations were built on the Atlantic coast by the turn of the century. By 1820, when the Secretary of the Treasury assigned the Fifth Auditor, Stephen Pleasonton, the "care and superintendence of the lighthouse establishment," 55 light stations existed along America's coasts. During Pleasonton's tenure from 1820 until 1852, the number of lighthouses (and lightships) increased to 325.[2]

Few systematic records of keeper appointments exist before 1828. Any attempt to peer back into history and summon up the women who might have been keeping lighthouses at the turn of the nineteenth century is obscured by gaps in the historical records—gaps that reflect the lack of interest in recording the accomplishments of working men and women in that period. After 1828, "Lighthouse Keepers and Assistants" in the National Archives—seven hand-written ledgers that served as the official record of lighthouse keeper appointments and salaries between 1828 and 1905—reveals the names of at least 122 women who were appointed official keepers in their own name. Twice that number were officially appointed assistant keepers, generally aiding their fathers or husbands. A great many more women never received official appointments, but kept a light for a few months after a husband's death—until a new keeper arrived at the station.

Until now, few sources have recorded the experiences of these women. Much of the published literature about women in the nineteenth century focused on prescriptions for proper female behavior, expressing social norms formulated largely by men. Their writings described the ideal female, emphasizing the passivity of her nature and her domestic attributes, and focused on middle- and upper-class, white, northern, urban women. The actual experiences of women who were forced by circumstances to earn their own living, of immigrant women, and of black women bore no relation to those established norms.[3]

Because writers of the time did not feel that the activities of working women were exemplary, very few noted their accomplishments. Actually, the same can be said for blue-collar working-class men. Not until the twentieth century do we find male lighthouse keepers sharing their personal experiences on the job. The men and women who kept the lights were, by and large, not drawn from a class that recorded their activities. Only when newspaper journalists picked up the drama of fierce storms or perilous rescues or unusual careers were the acheivements of either sex made a matter of permanent record.

The written record is far more complete regarding the construction and maintenance of the light stations because of annual reports published by the U.S. Light-House Board (which administered lighthouses from 1852 until 1910) and periodic reports about the conditions at the stations by the inspectors who regularly visited the light stations. Other than the appointment records and the 10-year census, lighthouse keepers become known mainly through secondary sources—obituaries and newspaper articles focused on dramatic episodes or unusually long careers. Personal histories may have been handed down orally within families, but those are largely lost to us now.

⋙⋘

[1] National Archives, Record Group 26, Entry 17H, "Draft Copies of Letters Sent, 1813-1852."

[2] Candace and Mary Louise Clifford, *Nineteenth-Century Lights: Historic Images of American Lighthouses* (Alexandria, Virginia: Cypress Communications, 2000), p. 21.

[3] See Carol Ruth Berkin and Mary Beth Norton, *Women in America: A History* (Boston: Houghton Mifflin Co., 1979) for further information, particularly Part III: "Nineteenth Century America—the Paradox of 'Women's Sphere.'"

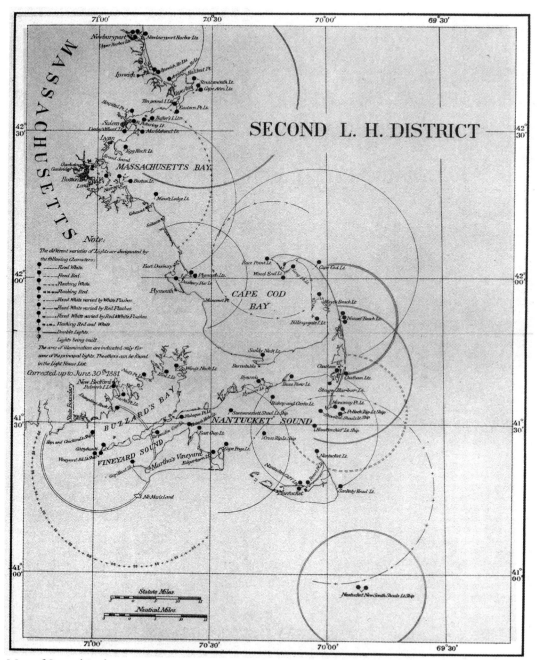

Map of Second Light-House District taken from the 1881 Annual Report of the Light-House Board. *The 13 maps in the 1881 report show 590 light stations in the United States. In 1881 at least 21 of these, or 3.5 percent of the total, had officially appointed female head keepers.*

HANNAH THOMAS

II. HANNAH THOMAS AT GURNET POINT LIGHT STATION, MASSACHUSETTS, 1776-1786

A point of land known as the Gurnet at the entrance to Plymouth Harbor in the Massachusetts Bay Colony belonged to John and Hannah Thomas of nearby Kingston. In 1768 the Thomases agreed to a request from a committee appointed by the General Court of Massachusetts to build and support a lighthouse on their land. A deed executed on November 23, 1768, and recorded in Plymouth County courthouse on February 23, 1769, spelled out the agreement.[1]

It appears that John Thomas assumed keeper's duties for the lighthouse built on his land. In 1771 he signed an account[2] of expenses for Gurnet Light House for the period of November 14, 1770, to November 14, 1771. The account included "40 measures of cotton weak [wick] yarn, £6.13.4; 50 measures of Candles, £1.13.4; one Lanthorn, 6 shillings; Carting out of sundry items, £1.3; and a tin pail for carrying oil, 8 shillings."

The outline of John Thomas's life is found in a biographic sketch written in 1889.[3] Born in 1725, Thomas studied medicine and practiced in Kingston, Massachusetts. He served with colonial militia regiments between 1746 and 1760, then returned to his practice in Kingston until 1775. He then raised a regiment of volunteers and was appointed a brigadier-general. During the siege of Boston his fortification of Dorchester Heights led the British to evacuate. Promoted, he was given command of the colonial army in Canada, where he died of smallpox in June 1776.

Gurnet Point Light became his wife's responsibility when General Thomas went off to war. In Hannah's era the lighthouse keeper's job was a seven-day-a-week responsibility. The two lamps in each lantern at Gurnet Point had to be lit and kept burning every night of the week, every day of the year. By 1775 the tallow candles used in the earliest lanterns in the colonies had been abandoned, for their light was too feeble to be visible from any distance. Four flat-wick lamps (also called bucket lamps) were used at Gurnet Point, without any reflecting apparatus, each having four large wicks.

The lamps burned whale oil, which gave off a large amount of smoke and soot, dimming the light and hazing over the glass around the lantern. The oil in the lamps had to be replenished two or three times during the night, the wicks trimmed, and the glass wiped clean. At dawn, the lamps were extinguished and cleaned.

Hannah saw to it that the Gurnet Light was tended during the first year of her husband's absence. The legislative records of the Massachusetts Bay Council contain her petition "praying for an allowance [for keeping] the Light House on the Gurnet at the entrance [of Plymouth] Harbour one year five months and Nine days [ending the] 23 Day of April 1775 at which time the Lights were Extinguished,"[4] presumably until the war ended.

❧

The American colonists were very dependent on the sea, not only for traveling from place to place, but for fish to eat and for transporting supplies and manufactured goods along the coast and to and from Europe. Ship captains had such a dire need for landmarks, both in daylight and darkness, to tell them their location and guide them into safe havens along the coasts and waterways, that they paid harbor fees to finance lighthouses or established lotteries to raise the necessary money to erect them.

The colonists who declared independence in 1776 had no navy— a disadvantage from which they suffered throughout the Revolutionary War. Sailing ships of the British Royal Navy, armed with cannon, prowled up and down the coast to harass, give chase to, and capture unarmed commercial vessels whenever they found them. The calculating eyes of British naval commanders must have studied the lonely lighthouses that marked the hazards and harbors along the

Nineteenth-century twin towers at Gurnet Point in Plymouth Harbor. When John Thomas went off to war in 1776, his wife Hannah was left with responsibility for his lighthouse. She remained in charge until 1786. Courtesy of the National Archives, #26-LG-7-11.

Atlantic coast. If those landmarks could be put out of commission, or better still, destroyed, then the commercial ships of the rebellious colonists would be far more vulnerable to British attack.

The residents of the three small towns on Plymouth Bay—Plymouth, Duxbury, and Kingston—knew that the small towers at Gurnet Point were in danger, so they threw up earthworks and built a crude fort around them to protect them from the guns of British ships. The colonists must certainly have watched with dismay when in 1778 the British frigate *Niger*, maneuvering just offshore, went aground on the shoals of Brown's Bank. In the gun battle between the stranded frigate and the colonists defending Gurnet Point, a wild shot from the ship pierced the walls of Gurnet lighthouse, but the twin lanterns at either end of the building were not damaged.

A "History of Plymouth (Gurnet) Light, Massachusetts" (author and source unknown) on file in the National Archives states that in 1778 the armed brigantine *General Arnold* was caught in a blizzard while less than a mile from the light and the captain anchored his vessel rather than risk the treacherous water of Plymouth's inner harbor without a pilot. The vessel dragged anchor and hit on White Flats. Seventy-two of the crew died, most of them freezing to death in the below-zero temperature before they could be rescued. . . . The Keeper of Gurnet Light [presumably whoever was living in Hannah Thomas's house at the time] was unable to go to their aid because the harbor was blocked with ice. A causeway had to be built over the ice to rescue the survivors.

Repairs to the keeper's dwelling on Gurnet Point were not made until 1783, two years after the war ended. On July 2, 1783, the Massachusetts legislature passed a resolution in response to a petition from Hannah Thomas regarding keeping of the lighthouse on Gurnet Point. In the February session in 1785[5] the legislature reiterated that "the offer, benefit and privileges of keeping and tending the light house on an island called the Gurnet, at the entrance of Plymouth harbor, is reserved to the said John, Hannah, and [son] John, owners of the said island, and their heirs and assigns."

In 1784 the May session of the Massachusetts legislature recorded Hannah Thomas's petition "praying that the barrack [erected] on her land at the Gurnet may be given to her for the damages done to her house, fences, etc., while a garrison was kept at that place." Her petition was granted.

Hannah, widowed and needing money to raise her children, thereafter may have done some of the light keeping herself; records for 1786, 1787, 1788, and 1789 show that she was paid £80 a year by the Massachusetts government.[6] She also hired male helpers. In 1786 one Nathaniel Burges signed a document, witnessed by John Thomas and Nathaniel Thomas [sons of General John Thomas] agreeing to "tend and keep the lighthouse situated on the Gurnet socalled, and at all proper times to light the lamps and keep the same lighted, in all respects faithfully to discharge the duty of a lighthouse keeper."[7]

Little more is known about Hannah Thomas, the first woman lighthouse keeper in the American colonies. Lighthouse historian Edward Rowe Snow said in his book *The Lighthouses of New England* that Hannah Thomas was still keeping the Gurnet Point Light Station when it was turned over to the federal government in 1790, but that may merely mean that she still owned the land, while Nathaniel Burges was hired to tend the light.

The ninth law passed by the new Congress in 1789 created the lighthouse establishment—one of the earliest public works in the new republic—and eventually placed it under the authority of an auditor in the Treasury Department. In 1790 the new federal government took over the 12 lighthouses on the Atlantic coast, including Gurnet Point and five others in Massachusetts. Many lighthouses after the war were put in the hands of veterans—mature and capable men who were eager to find good jobs. Every contract, large or small, as well as the appointment and salary of every keeper was personally approved by President Washington. On March 19, 1790, Superintendent of Lighthouses Benjamin Lincoln wrote Alexander Hamilton, Secretary of the Treasury, as follows:

> Mrs. Thomas, the widow of the late General Thomas, . . . has been considered the keeper of the lighthouse at Plymouth. The house stands on her land, which seems to be the reason why she was appointed the keeper of the light. The lighthouse stands on an island said to be about forty or fifty acres . . . of land. The man who keeps the lighthouse for her has trouble with the improvement of the island. This however, is a private bargain between Mrs. Thomas and the keeper.

John Thomas (son of Hannah and John[8]) went to superintendent Lincoln in 1790 asking for appointment as light keeper at Gurnet. Lincoln wrote the Secretary of the Treasury as follows:

> I have now with me Mr. Thomas, son of the late General Thomas, whose mother has the care of the lighthouse at Plymouth. When she was first appointed to that trust, he was a minor; otherwise he probably would have had the appointment himself. He is a young gentleman of good character and I think is a fair candidate for the appointment under the United states.[9]

In 1801 the lighthouse at Gurnet Point burned, and when the Treasury Department went to rebuild it, the secretary found that the land still belonged to the Thomas family. Correspondence in 1801 and 1802[10] from William Miller, Commissioner of the Revenue, to Benjamin Lincoln, Superintendent of Lights, gives the dimensions of the old light: "The old Light House was of Wood 30 by 18 feet and

A single tower stood at Gurnet Point in 1958, surrounded by traces of revolutionary War earthworks. Courtesy of the U.S. Coast Guard Historian's Office.

22 feet high, there were two lights raised 18 feet and Octagons at the ends of the Building," each of which contained two lamps—commonly referred to as "twin lights." The lanterns, which protected the lamps against the weather, were constructed of heavy wooden frames holding small, thick panes of glass. These twin lanterns were easily distinguishable from nearby Barnstable Light, and could be lined up by mariners, giving an exact location at that one point.

Commissioner Miller directed Lincoln to arrange the purchase of the land from John Thomas's heir(s). Congress appropriated $2,500 in 1802 to buy the land and erect a new lighthouse. The Thomas family received $120 for the land on which the lighthouse stood and for "Ground adjoining, as will be sufficient for Vaults and other appendages."[11] Nothing remains of the first light towers save the eroded earthworks of the long-abandoned fort, which are still visible near the surviving lighthouse, built with its twin in 1842. Although the need for twin towers was eventually eliminated by more efficient aids to navigation, twin lights were maintained at Gurnet Point long after most others were abandoned—until in 1924 one of them was discontinued and the tower removed. The second tower survives and was recently moved away from the eroding shoreline.

⦿

[1] From Richard M. Boonisar's collection on Hannah Thomas: a copy from the records and deeds for the County of Plymouth, book number illegible, folio 245, found in the National Archives, Record Group 26. We are much indebted to Mr. Boonisar, who owns property on Gurnet Point, for sharing his files on Hannah Thomas and thus allowing us to revise this chapter with more accurate and detailed information.

[2] From the Boonisar collection, no source listed.

[3] *Appleton's Cyclopedia of American Biography,* James Grant Wilson and John Fiske, editors (New York: D. Appleton & Co., 1889), Vol. VI, p. 84.

[4] Legislative Records of the Council, xxxviii, 278, Mass. Archives, ccxvii., 15, from Boonisar collection.

[5] Ibid., p. 886.

[6] In Boonisar collection, no source indicated; in a personal communication in September 2000, Boonisar indicated that he believed Hannah Thomas hired a caretaker to perform the keeper duties while she collected the salary.

[7] In Boonisar collection, no source indicated.

[8] According to Hannah Thomas's will, filed in the Plymouth County Court of Probate, July 5, 1819, she and John Thomas had three children—Hannah, John, and Nathaniel.

[9] National Archives, Entry 17A, "Letters Received by the Treasury Department, 1785-1812," Vol. 4, p. 17.

[10] National Archives, Record Group 26, "Lighthouse Letters, 1792-1809," Microfilm IDM63.

[11] Ibid.

1. New Lamps to Light the Atlantic Coast

As the new United States was coming into being, the flat-wick lamp was replaced in lighthouses by the spider lamp—a pan of oil with four or more wicks protruding from it. It had no chimney, and the acrid fumes given off by the spider lamp burned the eyes and nose, often driving the keeper out of the lantern housing. The intensity of the light depended on the lantern glass being kept clean and the wicks properly trimmed, and keepers became known as "wickies."

In 1812 the Argand lamp was introduced from England. This was a fountain lamp consisting of an oil reservoir, a burner with a hollow circular wick and lamp chimney, and a parabolic reflector. The new lamp was smokeless. Because oxygen passed both inside and outside the wick, the flame burned much more brightly—equivalent to the light of seven candles (candlepower). A reflector behind the lamp further increased its brightness. A lighthouse might use a chandelier with up to thirty of these lamps to provide adequate light.

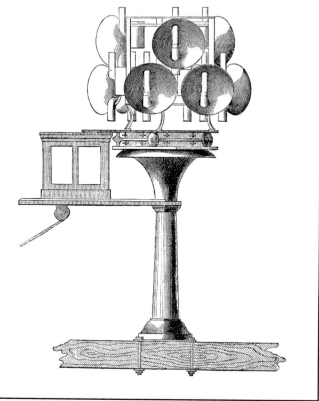

Illustration of a parabolic reflector system taken from M. Léonce Reynaud, Memoir Upon the Illumination and Beaconage of the Coasts of France.

III. CATHERINE MOORE AT BLACK ROCK HARBOR LIGHT STATION, CONNECTICUT, 1817-1878

Catherine (Kate) Moore did not become official keeper of the Black Rock Harbor Light Station on the north shore of Long Island Sound until 1871 when she was 76 years old. Her father, Stephen Tomlinson Moore sought the keeper's post decades earlier, in 1817, after injuries from a fall aboard ship kept him from going to sea on the vessel in which he had invested. In 1889 Kate told a reporter from the *New York Sunday World*, "I was just 12 years old when I first began to assist my father in trimming the wicks. A few years after that his health began to fail and from then on I was practically the keeper."[1] She did her invalid father's work and cared for him for 54 years.

Kate's is the first voice to come directly to us from the ranks of women who kept the lights. "It was a miserable [light] to keep going, nothing like those in use nowadays," she said of the fixed white light, which was 350 candlepower. "It consisted of eight oil lamps which took four gallons of oil each night, and if they were not replenished at stated intervals all through the night, they went out. During very windy nights it was almost impossible to keep them burning at all, and I had to stay there all night."

The light was located on Fayerweather Island, originally 200 acres of forest, but shrunk by erosion to three scraggly acres of tall grasses and ailanthus trees (planted by Kate), stretching like a snake from Seaside Park in Bridgeport, Connecticut. "On [calm] nights I slept at home, dressed in a suit of boy's clothes, my lighted lantern hanging at my headboard and my face turned so that I could see shining on the wall the light from the tower and know if anything had happened."

Black Rock Harbor Light Station off Bridgeport, Connecticut, around 1880. Kate Moore assisted her father there from 1817 until 1871, then acted as official keeper from 1871 until 1878. The 1823 tower still stands. Courtesy of the National Archives, #26-LG-11-3.

CATHERINE MOORE

If the light went out, Kate got up to tend to it. "Our house was forty rods from the lighthouse, and to reach it I had to walk across two planks under which on stormy nights were four feet of water. And it was not too easy to stay on those slippery, wet boards with the wind whirling and the spray blinding me."

Storms and gales were part of her life.

> The island has been ruined by gales a number of times. Every fifty years these great gales come, the waves dashing clear over the island, and on Jan. 19, 1820, the last of the old trees [on Fayerweather Island] was swept away. The lighthouse itself blew over once when I was there (September 22, 1821). It was a dreadful thing to have happen, for this was then the only light on the Connecticut side of Long Island—the only light between New Haven and Eaton Neck—and was of course of inestimable value to mariners. Sometimes there were more than 200 sailing vessels in here at night, and some nights there were as many as three or four wrecks, so you can judge how essential it was that they should see our light.

During her service at Black Rock Harbor Light Station, Kate Moore saved at least 21 lives. "I wish it had been double that number. Of course there were a great many others, washed up on the shore, half-dead, whom we revived, and they all stayed with us until they received means to leave. They used to eat our provisions and the Government never paid us a cent for boarding them."

Dead sailors washed up on the shore as well. "Hundreds!" Kate said. "We had to keep them, too, until the Government chose to dispose of them."

When asked whether she found the solitude of her life trying, Kate said that she had never known any other.

> I never had much time to get lonely. I had a lot of poultry and two cows to care for, and each year raised twenty sheep, doing the shearing myself—and the killing when necessary. You see, in the winter you couldn't get to land on account of the ice being too thin, or the water too rough. Then in the summer I had my garden to make and keep. I raised all my own stuff, and as we had to depend on rain for our water, quite a bit of the time was consumed looking after that. We tried a number of times to dig for water, but always struck salt.

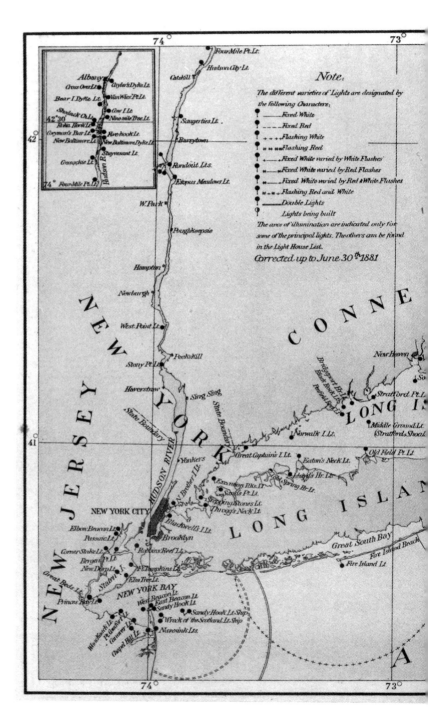

Note.

The different varieties of Lights are designated by the following Characters:

Fixed White
Fixed Red
Flashing White
Flashing Red
Fixed White varied by White Flashes
Fixed White varied by Red Flashes
Fixed White varied by Red & White Flashes
Flashing Red and White
Double Lights
Lights being built

The arcs of illumination are indicated only for some of the principal lights. The others can be found in the Light House List.

Corrected up to June 30th 1881

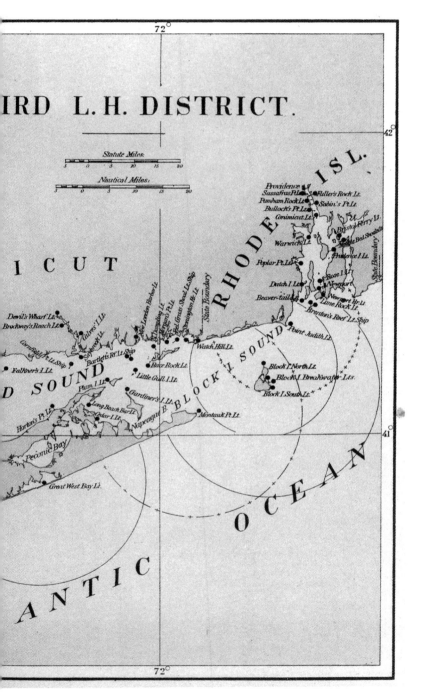

Statute Miles:

Nautical Miles:

RHODE ISL.

Providence
Sassafras Pt.
Pomham Rock Lt.
Bullock's Pt. Lt.
Conimicut Lt.

Fuller's Rock Lt.
Sabin's Pt. Lt.

Bristol Ferry Lt.
Mt. Bal. Seakli.

Warwick Lt.

Prudence I. Lt.

Poplar Pt. Lt.

Rose I. Lt.
Newport

Dutch I. Lt.

Beaver-tail Lt.

Newport Hr. Lt.
Lime Rock Lt.

Brenton's Reef Lt. Ship

Point Judith Lt.

Watch Hill Lt.

Devil's Wharf Lt.
Brockway's Reach Lt.

New London Harbor Lt.

Dumpling Lt.

Latimer's Pt. Lt.

Bartlett's Reef Lt. Ship
Stonington Hr. Lt.

Cornfield Pt. Lt. Ship

Talbot's I. Lt.

Saybrook Lt.

Bartlett's Rf. Lt. Ship

Little Gull I. Lt.

River Rock Lt.

Falkner's I. Lt.

Plum I. Lt.

D SOUND

Long Beach Bar Lt.

Gardiner's I. Lt.

Napeague B.

Horton's Pt. Lt.

Cedar I. Lt.

Montauk Pt. Lt.

Peconic Bay

BLOCK I. SOUND

Block I. North Lt.

Block I. Breakwater Lts.

Block I. South Lt.

Great West Bay Lt.

OCEAN

ANTIC

I C U T

State Boundary

State Boundary

Map of Third Light-House District from 1881 Annual Report of the Light-House Board.

2. Keepers in the First Half of the Nineteenth Century

Initially each keeper appointment and dismissal was approved by the President. As the number of lighthouses increased, first the Commissioner of the Revenue and later the Secretary of the Treasury would rely on the local customs collector to serve as superintendent of lighthouses and to recommend qualified candidates for appointments. Choices were often political. When a new party came into office, many keepers were replaced with citizens more sympathetic to the party newly in power.[1]

With a few exceptions, only one keeper was appointed per station; however, some keepers took it upon themselves to hire an assistant. The keeper's routine was to light the lamps at twilight, then trim the wicks between 11 and 12 that night. I.W.P. Lewis, engineer to the U.S. Light-house Survey, remarked that it was not uncommon for a light gradually to disappear between 3 and 4 a.m. He added, "The best keepers are found to be old sailors, who are accustomed to watch at night, who are more likely to turn out in a driving snow storm and find their way to the light-house to trim their lamps, because in such weather they know by experience the value of a light, while on similar occasions the landsman keeper would be apt to consider such weather as the best excuse for remaining snug in bed."[2]

As early as 1809, keepers were expected to keep records of their usage of oil, an increasingly expensive commodity in the 1800s. After the lighthouses were fitted up with Winslow Lewis's patented reflectors and lamps, a form was issued in 1813 to guide keepers in tracking their annual oil usage as well as supplies on hand and repairs needed.

According to the "Schedule of the Light Houses and Beacons in the United States," there were approximately 160 light stations in January 1833, exhibiting a total of 1,932 lamps.[3] With the increasing number of lighthouses, the need for more formal instructions soon became apparent. In April 1835, the Secretary of the Treasury wrote,

> The propriety of issuing a general letter or circular to each Lightkeeper, whether of House or Boat, instructing him in regard to the time of making light in the evening,—to his attention to the Light during the night, by trimming it, etc.,—to a judicious economy in the use and application of the oil, so as to produce the best light at the smallest expense,—to the necessity of strict care in respect to the cleanliness, order and safety of the lamps, reflectors, lens & other

machinery, and the importance of a careful supervision and preservation from fire and depredation of the property of the United States under his charge. The general course to be pursued in his sickness or absence, and in case of accidents might also be usefully prescribed. The sale of . . . spirits should be forbidden on the premises of the United States, and civility should be enjoined as a duty to strangers wishing to examine the Lights, and, in case of shipwrecks near, every practical effort required to be made to render reasonable and efficient relief, and

STATE OF *Maryland*

North Point LIGHT HOUSE,

June 3 1840.

RECEIVED of **GEORGE BANCROFT,** Superintendent of Light-Houses in Massachusetts, the following described Articles, for the use of the Light-House under my charge,—Viz:

Four hundred four _____ gallons of Spring Oil,

One hundred fifty eight do. Winter Oil,

Eight _____ gro. Wicks,

Seven 6/12 dozens of Tube Glasses,

One _____ Buffskin,

Fifteen _____ pounds of Whiting,

~~~~ ~~~~ ~~~~ _____ yards of Cotton Cloth,

Two _____ pair of Scissors,

for which I have this day signed duplicate receipts.

Miss Elizabeth Riley Keeper.

Witness *Jonathan Howland Jr.*

Receipt for supplies delivered in 1840 to Elizabeth Riley, keeper of the two lights at North Point Light Station, Maryland, from 1834 to 1857. Courtesy National Archives, Record 26, Entry 6, Box 2.

all due vigilance exercised to detect and expose every breech of the revenue laws in his neighborhood.[4]

Acting upon the Secretary's suggestion, Stephen Pleasonton, Fifth Auditor of the Treasury, issued the following instructions.

INSTRUCTIONS TO THE KEEPERS OF LIGHT HOUSES WITHIN THE UNITED STATES

1. You are to light the lamps every evening at sun-setting, and keep them continually burning, bright and clear, till sun-rising.

2. You are to be careful that the lamps, reflectors, and lanterns, are constantly kept clean, and in order; and particularly to be careful that no lamps, wood, or candles, be left burning any where as to endanger fire.

3. In order to maintain the greatest degree of light during the night, the wicks are to be trimmed every four hours, taking care that they are exactly even on the top.

4. You are to keep an exact amount of the quantity of oil received from time to time; the number of gallons, quarts, gills, &c., consumed each night; and deliver a copy of the same to the Superintendent every three months, ending 31 March, 30 June, 30 September, and 31 December, in each year; with an account of the quantity on hand at the time.

5. You are not to sell, or permit to be sold, any spirituous liquors on the premises of the United States; but will treat with civility and attention, such strangers as may visit the Light-house under your charge, and as may conduct themselves in an orderly manner.

6. You will receive no tube-glasses, wicks, or any other article which the contractors, Messr. Morgan & Co., at New Bedford, are bound to supply, which shall not be of suitable kind; and if the oil they supply, should, on trial, prove bad, you will immediately acquaint the Superintendent therewith, in order that he may exact from them a compliance with this contract.[5]

7. Should the contractors omit to supply the quantity of oil, wicks, tube-glasses, or other articles necessary to keep the lights in continual operation, you will give the Superintendent timely notice thereof, that he may inform the contractors and direct them to forward the requisite supplies.

8. You will not absent yourself from the Light-house at any time, without first obtaining the consent of the Superintendent, unless the occasion be so sudden and urgent as not to admit of an application to that officer; in which case, by leaving a suitable substitute, you may be absent for twenty-four hours.

9. All your communications intended for this office, must be transmitted through the Superintendent, through whom the proper answer will be returned.

Fifth Auditor and Acting Commissioner of the Revenue

TREASURY DEPARTMENT

FIFTH AUDITOR'S OFFICE

April 23d, 1835

⤙⤚

[1] Much of this sidebar is taken from Clifford, *Nineteenth-Century Lights*, pp. 74-76.

[2] Report of I.W.P. Lewis in U.S. Light-House Establishment, *Public Documents and Extracts from Reports and Papers Relating to Light-Houses, Light-Vessels, and Illumination Apparatus, and to Beacons, Buoys, and Fog Signals, 1789-1871* (Washington, D.C.: Government Printing Office, 1871), p. 370.

[3] National Archives, Record Group 26, Entry 6, "Annual Reports, 1820-1853."

[4] National Archives, Record Group 26, Entry 17K, "Letters Received from the Secretary of the Treasury," 1835.

[5] Several years later, Pleasonton struck out No. 6 of the Instructions and modified No. 7 to replace "contractors" with "Superintendent."

Rebecca Flaherty went with her husband to the Florida Keys when he was assigned to keep the first tower at Dry Tortugas on Garden Key in 1826. Courtesy of U.S. Coast Guard Historian's Office.

# IV.	REBECCA FLAHERTY AT SAND KEY LIGHT STATION, FLORIDA, 1830-1837

Rebecca Flaherty was a frequent letter writer. In 1824 she wrote a long letter to Stephen Pleasonton seeking a keeper's appointment for her husband John.

> My husband can produce the strongest recommendations from Baltimore to you, and I presume has as great a claim on his country as any candidate . . . He served his Country in the hour of danger and more particularly in the glorious defense of Baltimore [in the War of 1812]. He is now, from frequent attacks of rheumatism, rendered incapable of providing for his family the necessities of life and as the Southern climate is recommended to him for his complaint, if the light house at Pensacola is not engaged to any person . . . it will be gratefully received, or any other light house . . .[1]

In 1825, appointments of lighthouse keepers were still submitted to the President of the United States for approval. That year Rebecca wrote a long letter (apparently not her first) to Mrs. Adams (presumably the wife of President John Quincy Adams), as follows:

> Sensible of your philanthropy, I presume once more to trouble you respecting a situation for my husband. There is a light house at Thomsons Point near Annapolis that is nearly ready for the keeper to go into, and if you would please to grant us your interest with Mr. Stephen Pleasonton, the 5th auditor, I feel confident we could obtain the situation. My husband can get letters here from gentlemen of the first standing, and if you will kindly condescend to give him a letter, that alone would have much more weight than all the rest.[2]

What action Mrs. Adams took is unknown, but lengthy correspondence in the National Archives indicates that Major John Flaherty of Baltimore was appointed keeper of the light at Dry Tortugas in Florida in the spring of 1826.[3] Letters were exchanged about his transportation to his new post. A revenue cutter was sent from Delaware Bay to Baltimore to carry his family and household effects, and when the latter proved too extensive to fit in the cutter, a commercial vessel was chosen to move the remainder. Flaherty was instructed to draw advance salary from the Superintendent of Lighthouses in Key West.

By November of that year, Pleasonton learned from Mrs. Flaherty's sister that the Flahertys had problems. He reported to the Secretary of the Treasury that

> they are really destitute of all the necessities of life, and . . . they have not the means, of themselves, to obtain a supply to relieve them from a situation so disturbing and appalling. I have respectfully to request that you will give orders to the Revenue Boat on the Charleston station, to proceed forthwith to the Dry Tortugas, with such articles of provisions & stores, for their immediate use and preservation. I have further to request that in case the Keeper and his family should be desirous of relinquishing the situation, the Cutter should be ordered to receive them and their effects on board, and convey them to Baltimore . . .
>
> Whilst on this subject I consider it proper to observe that unless one of the Revenue Cutters can be employed in the Superintendence and supply of this Light House, & that at Cape Florida, at short intervals, it will be absolutely necessary to relinquish the Lights and abandon them; for it is utterly impossible for the Keepers to obtain provisions, and I have no means at my disposal with which to supply them.[4]

In 1827 the Flahertys must have felt somewhat less isolated when they were transferred to Sand Key Light Station, nine miles from Key West in Florida. John Flaherty took his wife and five children to live in the small house next to the light. The characteristic of the nearby Key West Light was fixed, so a revolving light was placed in the lantern at Sand Key atop a 70-foot conical brick tower. Fourteen lamps with 21-inch reflectors were hung on a chandelier, which on a clear night could be seen far out to sea. John Flaherty soon asked the superintendent in Key West to supply him with a boat for fetching supplies from the mainland.

Rebecca wrote a long letter to Stephen Pleasonton in 1828 informing him that her husband was ill with inflammation of the kidneys and should see a doctor; a six-month leave of absence was requested. She herself was not well. "The climate does not agree with either of us. I hope Sir, you will not think us whimsical, you were so kind as to have us moved to Sand Key to better our situation which it did, and nothing but the loss of our health could induce me to wish [John] to resign."[5]

Major Flaherty died at Sand Key in 1830 and was succeeded by his wife.

In 1833, Rebecca wrote the Secretary of the Treasury:

> I solicit your aid in correcting many of the grievances to which I am exposed in discharging [my] duties . . . First of all, I have to state that Sand Key is nine miles from Key West, and such is the violence of the seas for days and weeks together, as to render any intercourse with that place extremely precarious. A boat has generally been furnished by the Government for my use, but it has been constructed to draw too much water, the consequence of which has been to make it impossible to shelter it from the injury and damage which is effected by the commotion of the sea. On the East side of Sand Key there is a good harbour; which—if the Government would build a center board boat, drawing from six to nine inches water—would at all times, and during the greatest gale, protect it from all damage.[6]

She went on to say that the boat that had been supplied to her husband was too damaged to be used, "exposing her to starvation." In addition to needing a new boat, she asked that a man be hired to operate the boat and bring needed provisions from Key West. In the same letter she complained that though the government had furnished her firewood since 1827, a new regulation that prohibited the government from paying for her fuel was causing her hardship.

In 1831 an attorney in Key West, William Randolph Hackley, included in his diary a description of a visit he had made to Sand Key. He said that Rebecca Flaherty, her sister, and a hired man were the only inhabitants of the key, which he delineated as being 150 to 200 yards long and 50 yards wide[7]—the size of two football fields.

According to an article dated November 22, 1834, in *The Florida Herald*, a St. Augustine newspaper, Rebecca Flaherty married Captain Fredrick Neill. Rebecca Flaherty Neill remained keeper of the Sand Key light until 1837, when Captain Joshua Appleby took her place.[8]

---

[1] National Archives, Record Group 26, 17G, "Miscellaneous Letters Received (Numerical), 1801-1852."

[2] National Archives, Record Group 26, Entry 82.

[3] National Archives, Record Group 26, Entry 17H.

[4] Ibid.

[5] National Archives, Record Group 26, Entry 17F.

[6] Ibid.

[7] Love Dean, *Lighthouses of the Florida Keys* (Sarasota, Florida: Pineapple Press, 1998), p. 105.

[8] Ibid., p. 105-106. Several secondary sources incorrectly say that Rebecca Flaherty kept Sand Key Light Station until 1846 and that she and her children were swept away in the 1846 hurricane.

V. BARBARA MABRITY, 1832-1862, AND MARY ELIZA BETHEL, 1908-1913, AT KEY WEST LIGHT STATION, FLORIDA

In 1822 the federal government took possession of Key West.[1] A naval base was established there in 1823, and construction of a lighthouse was begun in 1825. Michael Mabrity, formerly a coast pilot, became its first keeper, earning $400 a year.[2] This was increased to $600 in 1828. His wife Barbara was his assistant. He continued to serve as a part-time harbor pilot and served on the town council in 1828.[3] He died of yellow fever in 1832, leaving Barbara with six children. Barbara took over his duties[4] and tended the 15 whale-oil-fueled lamps and reflectors until 1858, then a Fresnel lens until 1862, when she was 80 years old.

The early residents on Key West were in many ways pioneers. Indian wars in Florida between 1835 and 1842 caused enough skirmishes to prompt the Navy to strengthen its base on Key West. A road was built close to the lighthouse "to make it easier to spot possible Indians in the woods."[5] The road gave Barbara Mabrity quicker access to the town. In 1845 a fort, one of a string designed to protect the nation's major ports, was begun close to the lighthouse, giving Mrs. Mabrity a greater sense of security.

Nature, however, was the greater threat. Barbara Mabrity survived four hurricanes—in 1835, 1841, 1842, and 1846. The 1846 storm was described by U.S. Navy Lieutenant William C. Pease, who was aboard a small vessel in the harbor:

> The air was full of water, and no man could look windward for a second. . . . wrecks of all descriptions: one ship on her beam, three brigs dismasted, also three schooners; three vessels sunk, . . . four vessels bottom up. How many persons attached to these vessels

I am unable to say. We picked up only two. The lighthouse at Key West and Sand Key washed away, and Key West is in ruins. A white sand beach covers the spot where Key West lighthouse stood, and waves roll over the spot where Sand Key was.[6]

The first published history[7] of Key West in 1876 reported erroneously that "all the members of the keeper's family, seven in number..." died in the 1846 hurricane. This mistake has been repeated in numerous publications since; however, genealogist Sandra MacLean Clunies has conclusively proved that at least five of Barbara's children were married adults, were living elsewhere, and survived the hurricane. Mabrity herself was 64 years old at the time.[8] The lighthouse was destroyed and the new fort was swept away as well.

A new lighthouse was built on a hill farther inland and on higher ground,[9] and Barbara Mabrity lived and worked in the small, prefabricated, one-and-a-half-story wooden keeper's dwelling for another 16 years. In 1850 Barbara was given an assistant to help her with the buoys that had been placed on the treacherous reefs surrounding the island. In 1858 a third-order Fresnel lens with a single

The second tower for Key West Light Station was built in 1847. Shown here before it was raised 20 feet in 1894, the station, deactivated in 1969, is now a museum. Photo courtesy of U.S. Coast Guard Historian's Office.

BARBARA MABRITY AND MARY BETHEL

lard-oil-fueled hydraulic lamp with three circular wicks was installed, lessening the keeper's daily chore of cleaning lamps and reflectors.[10]

Key West was one of a few lights in Florida that remained lighted under Union control during the Civil War. In 1862, Barbara Mabrity was accused of harboring sentiments favoring the South and was encouraged to retire. She refused, and was then removed from her position. She died five years later at age 85.[11]

Barbara Mabrity was honored in 1999 when the Coast Guard named the second of a new series of keeper-class buoy tenders after her.

⚬⚬⚬

Many books say that William Bethel, who would become keeper at Key West in 1889, was Barbara Mabrity's grandson. Genealogist Sandra Clunies reports that 1880 census records indicate four William Bethels living in Key West at the time. Birth dates would indicate that the keeper with that name was not of Mabrity lineage.

What is certain is that Bethel had experience at several lights. He owned Indian Key, which served as construction headquarters for the men building Alligator Reef Light Station, and he was appointed assistant keeper when that station was activated in 1876. He later served at Dry Tortugas, becoming head keeper there in 1883. Presumably his family was with him. He was assistant keeper at Northwest Passage Light Station from 1886 to 1889, when he was transferred to Key West.[12]

In 1891 Bethel's wife, Mary Eliza, was appointed acting assistant keeper. In 1908 she was officially appointed keeper at Key West, while her son Merrill was appointed assistant keeper.[13] During the hurricane of 1909, William Bethel was injured in a fall while clearing the gutters of his house so that water running into the underground cistern would be clean. In a hurricane a year later, he went out into the storm, further injuring his health, and died six months later. In that same storm the glass in the lantern came crashing down just as Mary Eliza was about to climb the stairs in the tower. She remained at her post,

To be sent to the Light-House Board.

Office of Collector of Customs

At *Key West, Fla.*

Sept. 18", 1891.

To the Secretary of the Treasury,
       Washington, D. C.

    Sir:

      I have the honor to nominate Mrs. *Mary Eliza Bethel* for appointment as Acting *Assistant* Keeper of the Light-*House,* at *Key West Florida*, to take effect from date of entering on duty, in place of *Henry J Stanahan* who* *transferred*

                    Respectfully yours,

Approved.
23 Sept '91

                                    Collector of Customs and Superintendent of Lights.

EXTRACTS FROM LIGHT-HOUSE BOARD REGULATIONS.

    Superintendents of lights are to select keepers and assistants with particular reference to their fitness for and capacity to perform the duties required of them. Members of the keepers' family should only be nominated in rare and exceptional cases, where the interest of the service requires it.

    Keepers and assistants must be over eighteen years of age when appointed. They must be able to read and write, and in every respect be competent to discharge the duties of keeper. Assistants are required to observe the orders of the keepers in all matters connected with the duties of the establishment; and any disobedience of such orders will be held as a sufficient cause for recommending their discharge.

    Men of intemperate habits, and those who are otherwise mentally or physically incapable of performing the duties of light-keepers, must not be nominated for appointment.

    Keepers, when appointed, will receive instructions from the superintendent or inspector, as to the time of entering upon their duties, and will be paid at the rates stipulated in their appointments, from the date at which they actually enter upon their duties, and not before.

    * Here must be stated the manner in which the vacancy arises which this nomination is intended to fill. Thus: Resigned; deceased; or removed.

The first page of the nomination of Mary Eliza Bethel as assistant keeper at Key West in 1891. The form indicates her place of birth as the Bahama Islands and age as 37. The fine print indicates "Members of the keepers' family should only be nominated in rare and exceptional cases, where the interest of the service requires it." Courtesy National Archives, Record Group 26, Entry 28.

Mary Eliza Bethel served both as assistant and head keeper at Key West. Photo courtesy Monroe County Library.

with her son Merrill as her assistant, until 1913, when the light was automated.[14]

❧

[1] Thomas Taylor has published two extensive articles in *The Keeper's Log*: "The First Key West Lighthouse," spring 1995, and "the Second Key West Lighthouse," summer 1995. This chapter draws on these two articles.

[2] The correspondence regarding his appointment stated that "the President has appointed Michael Mabrity to be Keeper of the Light House at Key West." National Archives Record Group 26, Entry 17H. By the late 1820s, keeper appointments were no longer sent to the President. At that time the Secretary of the Treasury became solely responsible for approving appointments.

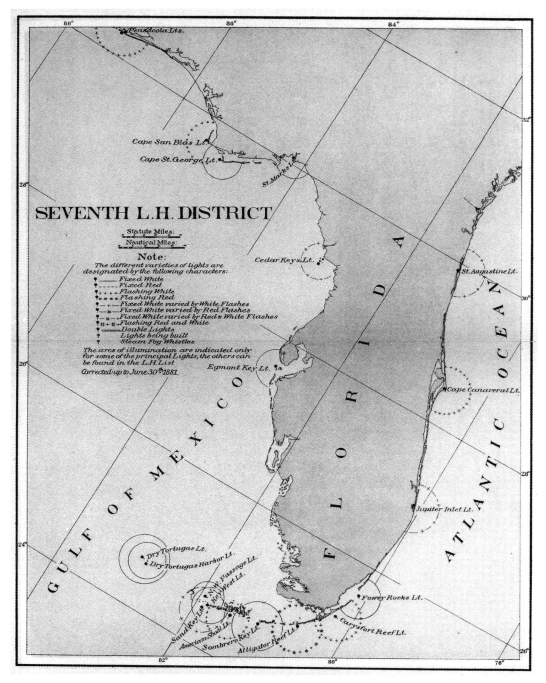

Map of Seventh Light-House District from 1881 Annual Report of the Light-House Board.

BARBARA MABRITY AND MARY BETHEL

[3] Dean, *Lighthouses of the Florida Keys*, p. 52.

[4] Correspondence regarding these appointments is found in National Archives, Record Group 26, Entry 17H.

[5] Thomas W. Taylor, "The First Key West Lighthouse," p. 19.

[6] Letter to Secretary of the Treasury, Washington, D.C., October 20, 1846, MCPL, quoted in Dean, p. 53.

[7] Walter C. Maloney, *A Sketch of the History of Key West Florida*, reprint (Gainesville: University of Florida Press, 1968), p. 41.

[8] Sandra MacLean Clunies, "Key West Lighthouse Keepers: New Findings from Public Records 1999," unpublished monograph used with author's permission.

[9] See Thomas W. Taylor, "The First Key West Lighthouse," pp. 16-22, and "The Second Key West Lighthouse," pp. 4-5.

[10] Ibid.

[11] Dean, *Lighthouses of the Florida Keys*, p. 57; Dean indicates that she was removed in 1864; other records indicate she was removed in 1862.

[12] Clunies, p. 9.

[13] *The Key West Citizen* of October 2, 1952, quoted in Dean, describes William Bethel's injury in 1909 and death in 1910, implying that Mary Eliza became keeper at that point; however, according to genealogist Sandra Clunies, microfilmed registers in the National Archives (Record Group 26, M1373) clearly show Mary Eliza's appointment as principal keeper on June 24, 1908, as well as her son's appointment as assistant keeper at that time.

[14] An article about the Mabrity and Bethel families at Key West Light Station appeared in the *Key West Citizen,* May 31, 1989. See also Dean, *Lighthouses of the Florida Keys*, p. 63.

Three women served as keepers of the Point Lookout Light Station, built on the Maryland side of the Potomac River in 1830. The station's first keeper, James Davis died soon after his appointment and was replaced by his wife Ann who served until her death in 1847. This 1883 view of the 1830 tower was taken by Major Jared A. Smith. Courtesy of the National Archives, #26-LG-24-5.

3. Other Female Lighthouse Keepers in the Early Nineteenth Century

One woman keeper, never appointed officially, must always remain nameless. The collector of customs in Key West wrote Fifth Auditor Stephen Pleasonton in 1826

> that Mr. DeBose, the Keeper [at Cape Florida Light] does not live in the dwelling attached to the Light House, nor has he for some time past, and that he has built a house on the mainland several miles from the Light House, and that he has given the whole direction of the Light to a black woman. . . . I may be permitted to say that the excessive hardships arising from sickness and the evils of a most horrid climate afford some palliation for his conduct.[1]

The isolation of the lighthouse at Pensacola, Florida, was outlined in a 1826 petition for an increase in salary for its keeper, Jeremiah Ingraham:

> His situation is so isolated and remote that he is necessarily deprived of the comforts of society, and is compelled to procure necessaries from Pensacola, a distance of nine miles, which subjects him to continual expense in boathire, as the heavy rains frequently render the land communication with the town impracticable. His salary . . . is 400 Dollars per annum and he is obliged to pay for the services of an assistant ten dollars per month, such aid being rendered indispensable to him by the complicated machinery of the Light-house requiring constant attention and cleaning.[2]

Doubtless his wife also performed many of the assistant's duties before his death. In 1840 the collector of customs wrote Stephen Pleasonton: "Mr. Ingraham, the keeper of the Light House at Barancas, died on Sunday the 6th inst. after a long and painful illness, during which time the superintendence of the light devolved on his wife, and has been well attended to. Mr. Ingraham's family are in a very helpless condition, and excites the sympathy of their friends."[3] He enclosed several letters and petitions from local people asking that Michaela Ingraham be appointed keeper. She was duly appointed and remained at Pensacola until 1855.

Even before the federal register of lighthouse keeper appointments was begun in 1828, Mrs. Edward Shoemaker took up her dead husband's duties at Old Field Point Light Station on the north shore of Long Island. She served only two years— 1826-1827, but Walter Smith, who followed her, died very soon after. The appointment of his wife, Elizabeth Smith, to replace him in 1830 is recorded in the register of "Lighthouse Keepers and Assistants," as well as in correspondence in the National Archives.[4] She kept the light for the next 26 years.

Lighthouse officials arrived unannounced. Sometime in the 1830s an inspector reported to the Secretary of the Treasury that he

> found the [Old Field Point] lighthouse in bad order. Mrs. Smith represents that she had then just been getting in her oil, and that it was unusually dirty, which I believe to be the fact from other testimony. . . . The Honorable Secretary will readily appreciate the difficulty of keeping in nice order any building under such circumstances, but more particularly a Light House, subject to the casualties of oil.

Mrs. Smith excused the chaos by telling the inspector that her house was "in a very dilapidated condition."[5]

Elizabeth Smith was succeeded by Mary Foster, who may have been her daughter, or another relative. A local newspaper, the *Long Island Star*, noted in 1869 that the Old Field Light had been in the care of the same family for over 40 years. Mary Foster was replaced that year, in spite of petitions signed by her friends, by a political appointee of the Grant administration.[6]

Also in 1830, Ann Davis succeeded her husband James as keeper of the Point Lookout Light Station at the entrance of the Potomac River in Maryland. He was the first keeper of that light, but died six months after his appointment. Ann's salary was $350, and her contract contained a notation forbidding the selling of liqueurs on the lighthouse premises. She served until her death in 1847.

In 1834 Elizabeth Riley was appointed keeper of the two lights at the North Point Light Station in Maryland and stayed at her post until 1857. In 1864 Keeper H. Schmuck was drafted by the military. The lighthouse inspector wrote Chairman Shubrick that he was "a valuable man to the Department, and if it is feasible to procure his exemption, it would no doubt advance its interests."[7] Schmuck apparently did not get his exemption, for his wife replaced him as keeper that year and kept the lights at North Point for the two years until his return.

The first keeper at Morgan's Point Light Station, Connecticut, was a Captain Daboll, who won contracts to build several of the lighthouses on Long Island Sound. He kept the light from 1831 until 1838, when he died, leaving his wife Eliza with six small children. (Women in the nineteenth century averaged six or seven children each.) Mrs. Daboll's reputation was such that her letter of appointment from Washington said that she "belongs to that class of citizens whose standing in society is of the first responsibility." So conscientious was she, in fact, that when her light failed one night, she walked to the ferry in Groton to report the situation to the authorities in New London before word could reach them from any other source.[8]

Political influence in keepers' appointments was widespread in the first half of the nineteenth century. A letter to the Secretary of the Treasury in 1845 mentions two candidates to keep the light at the mouth of Mahon's Ditch on Delaware Bay. "One is Capt. John Smith, the present incumbent, the other Mr. Thomas E. Harvey, of this place or neighborhood. Both Democrats and both, at the last election, supported and voted for the 'Polk electors.'"[9] Mr. Harvey got the job, but died a few years later. Petitions bearing dozens of signatures were submitted to the Secretary of the Treasury asking that Mrs. Susan Harvey be appointed to succeed her husband. She received the appointment; however, in 1851 Whig opponents circulated reports suggesting that Susan was not doing a good job. More petitions and two dozen letters supporting Mrs. Harvey, helped her to retain her position until 1853.[10]

Angeline Nickerson feared for the loss of her appointment at Chatham Light Station on Cape Cod in Massachusetts after the change in administration in 1849.

Chatham twin lights at the time they were kept by Angeline Nickerson, keeper from 1848 to 1862. Courtesy of the U.S. Coast Guard Historian's Office.

A letter written in her behalf to newly elected President Zachary Taylor pleaded her case:

> Upon the death of Mr. Simeon Nickerson the keeper of the "Chatham Lights," . . . in October last, Mrs. Angeline Nickerson his widow was appointed to fill the vacancy. Mr. N., it was admitted on all hands, had been a most attentive faithful and honest keeper and left at his decease, a destitute family. The appointment of his widow, so far as I know, gave general satisfaction. Of one thing, I am certain, which is, that she discharged the duties . . . in a most careful and faithful manner, and no charge of neglect or want of fidelity can be sustained against her. Having resided for forty years in the immediate vicinity, and in view of the Light, I can testify that it has never been in a better condition than since it has been under her charge, nor is there any Light upon the Coast superior to it.[11]

Angeline Nickerson succeeded in keeping her position until 1862. With four surviving children under the age of 12 to support, she would have been very thankful for the $400 per annum salary[12] for her keeper position.

Catherine Whittlesey kept the Lynde Point Light Station at Saybrook, Connecticut, from 1840 until 1852. In January 28, 1848, a letter to the Secretary of the Treasury reported "that the light at Saybrook was out . . . until 10 o'clock in the evening, the area then was very rough and many vessels were in danger of going ashore on account of the absence of the light." Keeper Whittlesey explained in a letter dated February 21 that

> the circumstances were as follows. The Lights were lit as usual at sundown, the oil then being in a fluid state, and for that reason I did not think it necessary to make a fire in the Lantern. At half past nine o'clock I perceived that the weather was much colder than it had been, and thinking it barely possible that the coldness of the weather might have some effect on the Lights, I went immediately outdoors to look at them, when to my astonishment I perceived they were out . . . I immediately carried up coals in a furnace, and with considerable exertion made them burn very well the remainder of the night.[13]

The collector of customs in New London supported her explanation.

Patty Potter succeeded her husband at Stonington Light Station, Connecticut, in 1842. Many other women keepers received glowing reports, but the one piece of information remaining about Patty Potter is negative. In October 1848 a lighthouse official reported that she "kept the most filthy house I have ever visited; everything appears to have been neglected." Lighthouse officials arrived unannounced. One can imagine a fastidious male catching a housewife/light keeper with dishes in the sink, children bickering, and beds unmade as she tended to the lamps and the lantern. In any case, Patty remained at her post until 1854.

❧

[1] Letter dated March 3, 1826, from Mr. Handy, U.S. Navy, to Stephen Pleasonton, found in National Archives, Record Group 26, Entry 17F, "Miscellaneous Letters Received (Alphabetical), 1801-1852."

[2] Ibid.

[3] National Archives, Record Group 26, Entry 82.

[4] National Archives, Record Group 26, Entry 17H, "Draft Copies of Letters Sent, 1813-1852"; many of the early letterbooks of correspondence burned in a 1922 fire, but these draft copies can, in some cases, reflect those that were lost.

[5] National Archives, Record Group 26, Entry 35, "Light-House Letters, 1833-1864."

[6] Personal communication with village historian of Old Field, 1991.

[7] Letter dated Sept. 24, 1864, from the Lighthouse Inspector to Chairman of the U.S. Light-House Board William Shubrick from National Archives, Record Group 26, Entry 24, "Letters Received from District Engineers and Inspectors, ca. 1853-1900."

[8] Information on lighthouses on Long Island Sound is found in Harlan Hamilton, *Lights and Legends* (Stanford, Connecticut: Westcott Cove Publishing Company, 1987).

[9] National Archives, Record Group 26, Entry 82.

[10] Ibid.

[11] Letter dated April 11, 1849, from Joshua Nickerson, found in National Archives, Record Group 26, Entry 35.

[12] National Archives, Record Group 26, "Registers of Lighthouse Keepers," M1373, R1.

[13] National Archives, Record Group 26, Entry 35.

Bombay Hook Light Station in 1897. Courtesy of the National Archives, #26-LG-10-13B.

MARGARET STUART

VI. MARGARET STUART AT BOMBAY HOOK LIGHT STATION, DELAWARE, 1850-1862

No words come directly from Margaret Stuart, who kept the Bombay Hook Light on the south side of the Smyrna River near the shore of the Delaware River from 1850 to 1862. The lighthouse—a white brick, two-story dwelling surmounted by a short tower and lantern room in the center of the roof—was built in 1831, rebuilt in 1841. Its first keeper was Duncan Stuart, Margaret's father. The appointment passed to Margaret in 1850. The lighthouse inspector reported in 1851 that Stuart (he spelled the name "Stewart," but Margaret's official appointment in "Lighthouse Keepers and Assistants" lists her as Margaret Stuart) was 89 years old, and that his daughters did the actual work of keeping the station "neat and clean."

The inspector's report indicated that the Stuarts were tending Argand lamps under rather difficult conditions:

> Reflectors of thin copper and a very thin film of silver-plating, much worn off in spots; not firmly placed on the frame, and easily put out of adjustment. Lantern small, glass 8 x 12 inches; sashes thick and black—want painting very much; the frame of the dome and the lantern very dirty for want of paint, lantern leaks very much; until rebuilt, leaked in every part of building; tower so open it is difficult to carry a light into the lantern; wood-work rough and not planed; floor of lantern coppered; no curtains allowed; Captain Howard tinkered up the lamps and burners in May; four spare lamps, burners very common.

The inspector reported that Mr. Stewart had the lighthouse whitewashed at his own expense because there was no allowance for lime for whitewashing. The report made the dwelling sound rather primitive:

House wants painting; spouts, etc., rusty for want of paint. Roof of the house very open—places a quarter of an inch between the shingles, brick-work rough; floors not tongued and grooved; rough and open in the attics; garret rooms not plastered; wooden pillar, supporting steps, much worm-eaten; cellar in bad order—wants cementing and repairs; kitchen in cellar; oil smells baldly [sic].

In 1855 the *Annual Report of the Light-House Board* indicated that "new iron lanterns for fourth-order apparatus have been substituted for the old and defective style hitherto in use," and "superior French plate glass of very large dimensions" installed in the lantern. These should have made Margaret's duties a little less onerous.

Margaret Stuart's appointment ended, as did those of many other lighthouse keepers, during the Civil War. Many lights were extinguished then to prevent their aiding the enemy, and the confusion of the period disrupted the careers of many keepers.[1]

The Bombay Hook Light was discontinued in 1912.[2] In 1974 it was either destroyed by fire or demolished as a hazard, with only the foundation remaining. The site is now the property of the U.S. Fish and Wildlife Service and is part of the Bombay Hook Wildlife Refuge.

[1] Information is taken from Robert deGast, *The Lighthouses of the Chesapeake* (Baltimore: Johns Hopkins University Press, 1973), and annual reports of the Light-House Board located in Record Group 26 at the National Archives, Washington, D.C.

[2] U.S. Fish and Wildlife Service, *A Brief History of Bombay Hook National Wildlife Refuge* (Smyrna, Delaware).

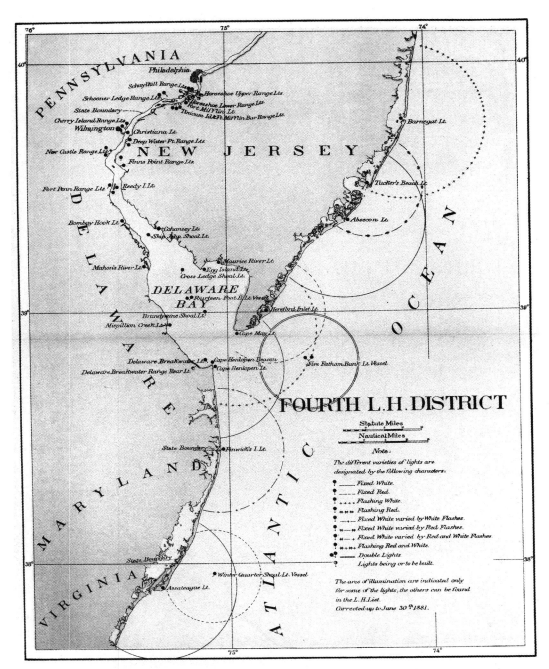

Map of Fourth Light-House District from 1881 Annual Report of the Light-House Board.

4. A Dangerous Occupation

Tales of tragedy were all too common in the lighthouse service. In 1718 the first keeper of the Boston Harbor Light, George Worthylake, was rowing his wife and daughter, along with a friend and a slave, between shore and the island in Boston Harbor where the light stood, when their dory capsized in heavy seas. All were drowned—a foretaste of the many dangers to be faced by those who kept the lights. This incident made such an impression on a 13-year-old named Benjamin Franklin that he wrote a ballad—"The Lighthouse Tragedy"—which he printed and hawked on the streets of Boston, with great success.

Lighthouse keepers in the eighteenth and nineteenth centuries, male and female, faced much danger and performed heavy physical labor. Ida Lewis at Lime Rock Light Station, Kate Walker at Robbins Reef Light Station, and Margaret Norvell at Port Pontchartrain Light Station (there may have been others we do not know about) launched wooden dinghies to make daring rescues of shipwrecked mariners. Several women keepers—Abbie Burgess at Matinicus Rock Light Station, Maria Younghans at Biloxi Light Station, Barbara Mabrity at Key West Light Station, and Harriet Colfax at Michigan City Light Station—are known to have stayed at their posts to keep the lights burning through terrifying storms and hurricanes.

Although women were generally not appointed to keep lighthouses in remote or dangerous locations, the nature of the work brought its own hazards. Cornelius Maher, keeper of the Oyster Beds Beacon on the north side of the Savannah River channel, drowned in 1853 while attempting to tow a brig to the city. His wife Mary kept the beacon for the next three years. Charles Anderson, keeper of the Round Island Light Station in Pascagoula, Mississippi, drowned in 1872. His wife Margaret assumed his duties and continued as keeper until her death in 1881. Then her daughter Mary kept the lights burning for four months, until a new keeper was appointed.

Melissa Holden, wife of the keeper of the Deer Island Thoroughfare Light on Mark Island on the Penobscot Bay coast of Maine, delivered her fifth child in the 1870s with the help of her other four children when her husband was away on the mainland. On another occasion when her husband was away in Rockland, Melissa detected the sound of muffled oars as prowlers landed on the shore. When she heard the intruders under her bedroom window, she doused them with the contents of her chamber pot—successfully discouraging any further mischief. When

Samuel Holden died in 1874, Melissa applied for and was granted his appointment, but two years later was replaced by a male keeper. She then moved ashore, remarried, and had several more children, whose descendants still live in Stonington, Maine.[1]

⌘

[1] Clayton H. Gross, "Lighthouses of Penobscot Bay—Mark Island," in *Island Advantages,* March 15, 1990.

Mary Anderson became keeper of the Round Island Light in Pascagoula, Mississippi, after her husband drowned in 1872. Courtesy of the National Archives #26-LG-37-60.

The cover of Harper's Young People: An Illustrated Weekly, *May 2, 1882, is of a fictional character that may have been inspired by Abbie Burgess, who assisted her father in keeping the lights at Matinicus Rock. Courtesy of The Library of Virginia.*

VII. ABBIE BURGESS GRANT AT MATINICUS ROCK LIGHT STATION, 1853-1872, AND AT WHITEHEAD LIGHT STATION, MAINE, 1875-1892

Abbie Burgess, who at age 14 moved with her family to the light station on Matinicus Rock off the coast of Maine, helped her father tend 28 Argand lamps. Her father won his appointment in 1853 and took with him his invalid wife and children—one son, Benji (who was generally away on fishing boats), and four daughters (of whom Abbie, born in 1839, was the eldest).

Matinicus Rock is a lonely, barren outcropping four miles off the south end of Matinicus Island. Twenty miles distant from the mainland, the original light station included two wooden towers for the lamps, attached to either end of the rectangular rubblestone keeper's dwelling. Like many light stations, Matinicus Rock had small structures for a fog bell and other equipment, and perhaps even domestic animals. Sheds housed coal to provide heat, the oil used to fuel the lamps, and lifeboats. A cistern or rain shed collected fresh water.

The island's surface was a confused plain of loose stones and boulders, many of which moved when the waves swept over them at high tide. A boat slip with rails and winch was needed to launch a lifeboat and unload supplies. According to the 1891 *Annual Report of the Light-House Board*, "There is a little cove where material can be hauled up in pleasant weather, but it has no harbor. The lighthouse keeper effects a landing by steering his boat through the breakers on top of a wave, so that it will land on the boatways, where his assistants stand ready to receive him and draw his boat so far up on the ways that a receding wave cannot carry it back to the sea."

The keeper's job revolved around maintaining the lamps, the twin towers[1] (built of stone in 1848), and the quarters. During the early 1800s, lighthouses used lamps that burned whale oil. A thick strain of whale oil was used in the summer, a thinner strain in the winter. In winter temperatures, even the thinner oil tended to congeal, forcing the keeper either to carry heated oil to the lantern or to keep a fire burning in a warming stove in the lantern of the lighthouse. The quality of the light depended on how well the wick was trimmed. All the accumulated soot had to be polished off the dustpans (reflectors) every day so that they would reflect the maximum light. The reliability of the lights was of great concern to keepers and mariners alike, for ships navigating perilous coasts in the eighteenth and nineteenth century depended on the lights to warn them away from danger. Sailors in those days still relied on the sun, stars, and primitive compasses to find their way, combining their knowledge of the tides, wind direction, water surfaces, cloud formations, and bird behavior to predict weather. Barometers of the time were crude kettle-shaped affairs in which the water level spilled over as pressure increased.

Rocks and shoals were extreme hazards in heavy weather as sailing ships sought their ports. Any failure of a light for even a short time could lead to disaster. Abbie learned to light the 28 Argand lamps that warned ships away from the dangerous ledges of Penobscot Bay and took her turn tending the lights and the stove during the night, permitting her father to spend part of his time fishing for lobsters and sailing to Rockland to sell them.

In January 1856 supplies were running desperately low because the lighthouse tender, which brought supplies twice a year, had failed to make its regular September call. Keeper Burgess decided to make a trip to Matinicus Island, five miles away,[2] to fetch food for his family and medicine for his sick wife. His son was away fishing, so Abbie was left in charge of the lights. Soon after Burgess left, a storm blew in out of the northeast, and he was unable to return for four weeks. Sheets of spray crashed over the island, followed by sleet and snow. As the violence of the gale increased, Abbie moved her mother and younger sisters into one of the two light towers. Finally, at high tide, the waves washed completely over the island, destroying the old keeper's quarters. The women watched the destruction from the tower.

Many of the men and women who kept the lights had awesome tales to tell of the isolation of a lighthouse (particularly on remote islands), of the tedious daily tasks that kept the keeper tied to the post, of the personal danger of keeping the light during storms, of perilous rescues of wrecked seamen. Abbie Burgess, in a letter to a friend, gave a detailed description of that terrifying and exhausting month:

> You have often expressed a desire to view the sea out upon the ocean when it was angry. Had you been here on the 19 January, I surmise you would have been satisfied. Father was away. Early in the day, as the tide rose, the sea made a complete breach over the rock, washing every movable thing away, and of the old dwelling not one stone was left upon another of the foundation.
>
> The new dwelling was flooded and the windows [shutters] had to be secured to prevent the violence of the spray from breaking them in. As the tide came, the sea rose higher and higher, till the only endurable places were the lighttowers. If they stood we were saved, otherwise our fate was only too certain.
>
> But for some reason, I know not why, I had no misgivings and went on with my work as usual. For four weeks, owing to rough weather, no landing could be effected on the Rock. During this time we were without assistance of any male member of our family. Though at times greatly exhausted by my labors, not once did the lights fail. Under God I was able to perform all my accustomed duties as well as my father's.
>
> You know the hens were our only companions. Becoming convinced, as the gale increased, that unless they were brought into the house they would be lost, I said to mother: "I must try to save them." She advised me not to attempt it. The thought, however, of parting with them without an effort was not to be endured, so seizing a basket, I ran out a few yards after the rollers had passed and the sea fell off a little, with the water knee deep, to the coop, and rescued all but one. It was the work of a moment, and I was back in the house with the door fastened, but none too quick, for at that instant my little sister, standing at a window, exclaimed, "Oh, look! look there! the worst sea is coming!"

That wave destroyed the old dwelling and swept the Rock. I cannot think you would enjoy remaining here any great length of time for the sea is never still and when agitated, it roars, shuts out every other sound, even drowning our voices.

After the storm subsided, Abbie's father returned to find his family and the lights safe. A year later, under similar conditions, he was away from the rock for three weeks, but Abbie kept the lights burning. This time the family ran out of food supplies, and were down to one egg and one cup of corn meal a day when Burgess returned.

In 1857 new cylindrical granite towers, 48 feet tall, topped by lanterns in which third-order Fresnel lenses were installed, were constructed on Matinicus Rock. The height of a tower depended on a calculation of the distance at which the light must be visible. Those towers in exposed locations were designed to withstand wind, waves, current, and ice, and the stability of the tower needed to be carefully computed to make it safe under the most severe conditions.

Matinicus Rock Light Station on an island off the coast of Maine, where Abbie Burgess assisted her father from 1853 to 1860. One of the 1857 towers continues as an active aid to navigation, and the island, an important seabird nesting site, serves as a research headquarters for Audubon biologists. Courtesy of the U.S. Coast Guard Historian's Office.

The price of whale oil quadrupled about this time, prompting a search for an alternate fuel. When it was discovered that lard oil worked well when burned at a high temperature, the larger lamps were gradually switched from whale oil to lard oil.

Although Abbie's father lost his position to new Republican appointee, John Grant, in 1860, Abbie stayed on to assist the new keeper, then fell in love with his son. Abbie eventually married Isaac H. Grant, who became the assistant keeper at Matinicus on September 5, 1864. Abbie was appointed the third assistant keeper on November 9, 1870—one of over 240 women listed in "Lighthouse Keepers and Assistants" who served as assistant keepers between 1828 and 1905. She received $440 a year for her services.[3]

In 1869 a steam fog signal had been established on Matinicus Rock, probably prompting the creation of the third assistant position. Abbie had four children while stationed on Matinicus. She and her husband remained on Matinicus Rock until 1875, when they were transferred to Whitehead Light Station, near Spruce Head, Maine. Isaac was appointed keeper on April 28, 1875, and Abbie became his assistant on June 2, 1875. There Abbie's salary as assistant keeper was increased to $480 annually. Abbie and her husband served together as keepers at Whitehead until 1890, when her failing health led both of them to resign.[4] She died two years later, having spent 37 of her 53 years in lighthouses. Isaac lived until 1918.[5]

Shortly before her death, Abbie wrote her last letter:

> Sometimes I think the time is not far distant when I shall climb these lighthouse stairs no more. It has always seemed to me that the light was part of myself . . . . Many nights I have watched the lights my part of the night, and then could not sleep the rest of the night, thinking nervously what might happen should the light fail.
>
> In all these years I always put the lamps in order in the morning and I lit them at night. These old lamps on Matinicus Rock . . . I often dream of them. When I dream of them it always seems to me that I have been away a long while, and I am hurrying toward the Rock to light the lamps there before sunset . . . . I feel a great deal more worried in my dreams than when I am awake.

I wonder if the care of the lighthouse will follow my soul after it has left this worn out body! If I ever have a gravestone, I would like it in the form of a lighthouse or beacon.[6]

In 1945, many years after Abbie's death, lighthouse historian Edward Rowe Snow placed a miniature lighthouse on Abbie Burgess Grant's grave in Spruce Head Cemetery. Snow had for many years in the 1920s and 1930s flown his own plane to drop Christmas gifts by parachute to the lighthouse crews at offshore installations along the Maine coast. Abbie's story had obviously touched him.

In 1998 the Coast Guard commissioned the 175-foot buoy tender *Abbie Burgess* with an 18-man crew, which will service nearly 400 navigational aids from Pemaquid Point, Maine, to the Canadian border.[7]

Whitehead Light Station on Penobscot Bay in Maine, where Abbie Burgess Grant was official keeper from 1875 to 1892. The 1852 tower continues as an active aid to navigation. Courtesy of the National Archives, # 26-LG-4-37.

[1] A navigator could distinguish twin lights from a neighboring light station displaying a single beam. Several decades later, more sophisticated ways of distinguishing between lights were developed, and twin towers were no longer needed.

[2] Personal correspondence dated May 13, 1996, from Patricia Grant of Augusta, Maine, Abbie's great-granddaughter.

[3] *Register of Lighthouse Keepers, 1845 -1912* (National Archives, Record Group 26, M1373, Roll #1)

[4] Personal correspondence dated May 3, 1995, from David A. Gamage of Wilton, Maine, grandson of a keeper at Whitehead Light Station.

[5] Personal correspondence with Patricia Grant, May 13, 1996.

[6] Segments of Abbie Burgess's letters are quoted in several sources, including Ross Holland, Robert Carse, and Edward Rowe Snow.

[7] U.S. Coast Guard *First District News* press release No. 083-98.

Note:

The different varieties of Lights are designated by the following characters:

Fixed White
Fixed Red
Flashing White
Flashing Red
Fixed White varied by White Flashes
Fixed White varied by Red Flashes
Fixed White varied by Red & White Flashes
Flashing Red and White
Double Lights
Lights being built

The arcs of illumination are indicated only for some of the principal Lights, the others can be found in the L.H. List.

Corrected up to June 30th 1881

M A I N E

Bangor

Fort Point Lt.
Dice's Head Lt.
Pumpkin I. Lt.
Grindles Pt. Lt.
Negro I. Lt.
Indian I. Lt.
Goose I. Lt.
Saddleback Ledge Lt.
Brown's Head Lt.
Heron's Neck Lt.
Head Lt.
White Head I Lt.
Saquish Harbor Lt.
Matinicus Rock Lt.
Franklin I Lt.
Marshall's Point Lt.
Monhegan I Lt.
Bath
Burnt I. Lt.
Pemaquid Point Lt.
Hendrick's Head Lt.
Squirrel I. Lt.
Pond I. Lt.
Monhana I.
Portland
Breakwater Lt.
Portland Head Lt.
Halfway Rock Lt.
Cape Elizabeth Lts.
Wood I. Lt.
Goat I. Lt.
The Knubble Lt.
Boon I.Lt.
Portsmouth Harbor Lt.
Portsmouth
NEW HAMPSHIRE
Whale's Back Lt.
Isle of Shoals Lt.
Upper Harbor Lts.
Newburyport
Newburyport Hbr Lts.

ATLANTIC

FIRST

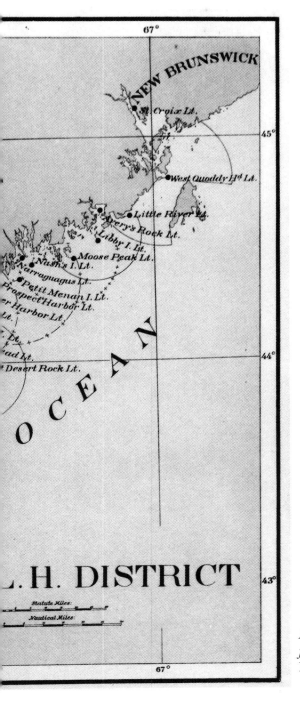

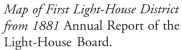

Map of First Light-House District from 1881 Annual Report of the Light-House Board.

5. Adoption of the Fresnel Lens

In 1822 a new and very superior lens was developed in France. Fresnel's circular glass lens surrounded the lamp, with prisms at the top and bottom to refract the light into a horizontal beam. The central prisms and drum (in the case of a fixed optic) or bull's eye (in the case of a rotating optic) also refracted the light into a horizontal beam, intensified by a powerful magnifying glass around the middle of the lens, resulting in a highly concentrated beam of light. In the case of a fixed lens, the light was concentrated into a 360-degree sheet of light. In the case of a rotating optic, the light was concentrated into beams, depending on how many flashes were employed.[1] The lens wrapped around a so-called mechanical lamp, which burned oil pumped up from a reservoir either above or below the level of the burner by means of weighted clock-works. Only one lamp was needed, with from one to five concentric wicks providing a great savings in oil consumption. The Fresnel lens came in six sizes at first, the largest giving off the powerful light needed on headlands or an open seacoast. Two more sizes were added. The smaller lenses were suitable for marking harbors, bays, or obstructions—places where the light did not need to be seen at great distances.

Although American sea captains travelling to Europe indicated that the Fresnel lens was far superior to the reflector system still in use in this country, it took many years for

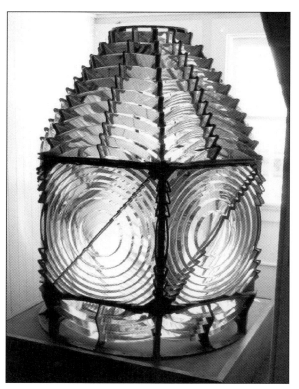

Fresnel lens on display at Hooper Strait Light, Chesapeake Bay Maritime Museum, St. Michaels, Maryland. National Park Service photo.

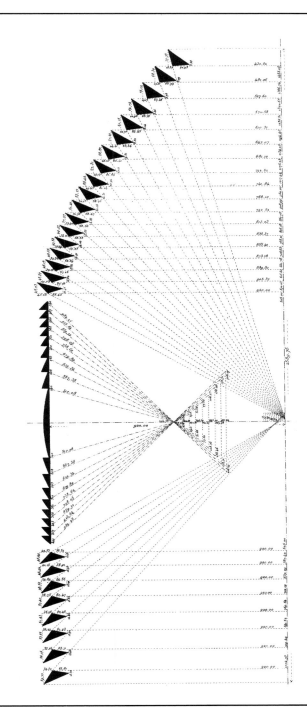

the United States to adopt the Fresnel lens in its lighthouses. The first Fresnel lenses in America were installed in the twin towers of Navesink Light Station on the New Jersey coast in 1840, but it was not until the U.S. Light-House Board took over the administration of lighthouses in 1852 that Fresnel lenses were uniformly installed in all new lighthouses. By the beginning of the Civil War, Fresnel lenses had replaced the reflector system in most active lighthouses.

∽≻○≺∼

[1] Personal correspondence with Wayne Wheeler of the United States Lighthouse Society dated January 4, 1993.

[2] See Connie Jo Kendall, "Let there Be Light," *The Keeper's Log*, Spring 1997.

Diagram showing how the elements of a Fresnel lens focus the light into a concentrated beam. As the lens rotates, the mariner sees a flash when the center of the bullseye (and its accompanying dioptic and catadioptric prisms) passes his view.[2] Taken from M. Léonce Reynaud, Memoir Upon the Illumination and Beaconage of the Coasts of France.

6. Creation of the U.S. Light-House Board

As maritime commerce increased and expanded into the Great Lakes, the Gulf of Mexico, and along the West Coast, many new lighthouses were built. Needless to say, administrative supervision by one man in the Treasury Department was no longer adequate to guarantee the efficient operation of so many aids to navigation. After a thorough investigation, Congress in 1852 created a lighthouse board to oversee the lighthouse service. The country was divided into 12 districts, with an inspector—a naval officer—and a district engineer—an army officer—for each.

The U.S. Light-House Board systematically worked for the improvement of aids to navigation, including the preparation of charts giving accurate locations and descriptions of lighthouses so that they might more easily be recognized, both as landmarks by day and as beacons at night. Attention was given to color characteristics of the lights and distinctive patterns of flashing. The strength of each light's illumination was measured. An annual *Light List* was published, describing all aids to navigation in the United States and detailing the distinctive characteristics of all lights and lighthouses.

Under the Light-House Board, the appointment of keepers was restricted to "persons between the ages of 18 and 50, who can read, write, and keep accounts, are able to do the requisite manual labor, to pull and sail a boat, and have enough mechanical ability to make necessary minor repairs about the premises, and keep them painted, whitewashed, and in order."[1] Keepers underwent a three-month probationary period before their full appointment was issued by the Secretary of Treasury. Keepers could be transferred between stations and districts. Young men with some sea experience were preferred as assistants at the larger stations, while retired sea captains or mates with families were frequently selected for stations with only one keeper. Stations with fog signals generally required an assistant with some experience as a machinist to operate the machinery and keep it in repair.[2] In 1867, an Act of Congress fixed the average annual salary of a lighthouse keeper at $600.[3]

Keepers were encouraged to cultivate the land associated with onshore stations and were forbidden to engage in any business that interfered with their presence at the station or with the proper and timely performance of their duties.

It was not surprising, however, to find a keeper working at his station as a shoemaker, tailor, or a justice of the peace. Keepers were not allowed to take in boarders nor were they given pensions or compensation for injury.

Inspectors visited the stations in their districts quarterly. They were to report on repairs needed to the tower and buildings; needed renovations and improvements; and the condition of the station, lantern, illuminating apparatus, and related equipment. The inspector was responsible for making sure the keeper understood the printed instructions for operating all equipment and other attendant duties. The inspector also reviewed the keeper's journal and records relating to expenditures, shipwrecks, and vessels passing. The inspector assessed the "attention of the keeper to his duties, and his ability to perform them well."[4] Both inspectors and engineers had authority to dismiss a keeper or other employee found in a state of intoxication.

Engineers superintended the "construction and renovation of the fixed aids to navigation in their respective districts."[5] The engineer or the inspector was responsible for acquiring information on the ownership of any potential site and reporting these details to the Board along with information about the topography of the site and the potential light's relationship with other lights and the water or hazard it was marking. When a tower was nearing completion, the engineer notified the superintendent of lights so that he could nominate the authorized number of keepers. In addition to nominating keepers, superintendents of lights were charged with paying salaries and disbursing other funds.

⋘⋙

[1] Arnold Burges Johnson, *The Modern Light-House Service* (Washington, D.C.: Government Printing Office, 1890), pp.102-103; this and the paragraphs that follow are taken from Clifford, *Nineteenth-Century Lights*, pp. 179, 184-186.

[2] Johnson, pp.103-105.

[3] George R. Putnam, *Lighthouses and Lightships of the United States* (Boston: Houghton Mifflin Co., 1933), p. 238.

[4] U.S. Treasury Department, *Organization and Duties of the Light-house Board; and Regulations, Instructions, Circulars, and General Orders of the Light-house Establishment of the United States* (Washington, D.C.: Government Printing Office, 1871), hereafter referred to as the *1871 Regulations*, pp. 54-55.

[5] Ibid., p. 57.

Biloxi Light Station on the Gulf of Mexico, kept by Mary Reynolds from 1854 to 1866, by Maria Younghans from 1867 to 1919, and by Miranda Younghans from 1919 to 1929. Courtesy of the National Archives, #26-LG-34-22A.

VIII. MARY REYNOLDS, 1854-1866, MARIA YOUNGHANS, 1867-1918, AND MIRANDA YOUNGHANS, 1918-1929, AT BILOXI LIGHT STATION, MISSISSIPPI

Women tended the light at Biloxi, Mississippi—the most prominent landmark on the Mississippi Gulf Coast—a total of 74 years. Mary[1] J. Reynolds was in charge from 1854 to 1866. She was followed by Maria Younghans, keeper from 1867 to 1918. Maria's daughter Miranda followed her and held her post until 1929. Although these three women racked up three-quarters of a century of continuous and dedicated service, almost no personal information about them survived their retirement, in part because they left no descendants to treasure their memories.

Built in 1847, the Biloxi tower was prefabricated of cast iron (possibly the first in the South to be so constructed), with a balustrade encircling the watch room, and was brought by ship to its permanent location along the roadbed of the Old Spanish Trail. Today the tower rests on a circular concrete base in the median of a major highway, U.S. 90, and is surrounded by a circular iron fence.

A sea wall was constructed in 1854 to protect the site from the tides and storms, and periodic repairs were required to keep erosion from tilting the tower. While the light itself stood 53 feet above the ground, its elevation put it 61 feet above sea level. The original illuminating apparatus consisted of nine cast brass lamps with separate reflectors. Its three-second flashing light marked the entrance to Biloxi Harbor for the many schooners that once plied the Mississippi Sound and Gulf waters in search of shrimp and oysters. It also welcomed those schooners seeking a lumber cargo on the Tchouticabouffa River and other inland waterways.

Mary Reynolds sought the aid of Mississippi's newly elected senator, Albert Gallatin Brown, to obtain her appointment in 1854 as second keeper of the Biloxi Light Station. Her annual salary was $400. When the Civil War broke out, the patriots of Biloxi wanted the light extinguished so that it could not aid Yankee ships, and Reynolds worried about her responsibility for the federal stores in her possession.

She turned to the governor for assistance in influencing the local men. Her letter is in the Mississippi Department of Archives and History.[2]

Biloxi, Nov. 26th, 1861

To His Excellency Gov. Pettus

Dear Sir,

With the request that you will pardon my informality in my letter, I beg to inform you that I am a woman entirely unprotected. I have for several years past been the Keeper of the Light House at Biloxi, the small salary accruing from which has helped me to support a large family of orphaned children.

These children being heirs at law to considerable property in Maryland, I have yearly received a stipend through the Hon. Henry May of Baltimore who is the Executor of their estates. Owing to our political rupture [the Civil War started in April 1861] I cannot hope for any immediate assistance from Mr. May.

I do not know if my [federal] salary as the Keeper of the Light House will be continued.

On the 18th of June last, the citizens of Biloxi ordered the light to be extinguished which was immediately done and shortly after others came and demanded the key of the Light Tower which has ever since remained in the hands of a Company calling themselves "Home Guards."

At the time they took possession of the Tower it contained valuable Oil, the quantity being marked on my books. I have on several occasions seen disreputable characters taking out the oil in bottles. Today they carried away a large stone jug capable of containing several gallons. They may take also in the night as no one here appeared to have any authority over them.

Their Captain, J. Fewell, is also Mayor of the City of Biloxi, and if you would have the kindness to write him orders to have the oil measured and placed under my charge at the dwelling of the Light House I would be very grateful to you for so doing.

I write to you merely as a Light Keeper believing that injustice has been and is still doing here. I can give you unquestionable reference as regards to my character.

I am a native of Baltimore and for many years a citizen of Mobile. Sad reverses of fortune and the care of so many orphan children of my deceased relatives rendered it necessary that I should exert myself to the uttermost for their support.

I have ever faithfully performed the duties of Light Keeper in storm and sunshine attending it. I ascended the Tower at and after the last destructive storm (1860) when men stood appalled at the danger I encountered.

After the Light was extinguished, I wrote to New Orleans and offered my services to make Volunteer Clothing [for Confederate soldiers]. Received a large bale of heavy winter clothing which I made during the hottest season of the year working day and night to have them done in time.

I do not speak thus of myself through vanity or idle boasting but to assure you that I have tried to do my share in our great and holy cause of freedom.[3]

The governor's reply is not available, but the mayor replied to the collector of customs on February 5, 1862, as follows:

At your request I have the honor to inform you that the Citizens of Biloxi in a public meeting resolved to remove the Reflector from the Light House at this place, and to take possession of the Oil in possession of the late Keeper, which was sold for the amount of Thirty Dollars which fund was distributed by me to the poor destitute families. The property which the Citizens have taken from the premises of the Light House is safely secured and is subject to the order of the authorities of the Confederate States Government.[4]

Reynolds was listed as official keeper until 1866—although the light may have remained dark until that year. Like many Southern keepers, she was paid by the Confederate Light-House Establishment during the war.[5] Reynolds name reappears in the records of the U.S. Light-House Board as keeper of the Pass Christian Light on the Mississippi Sound from 1873 to 1874.

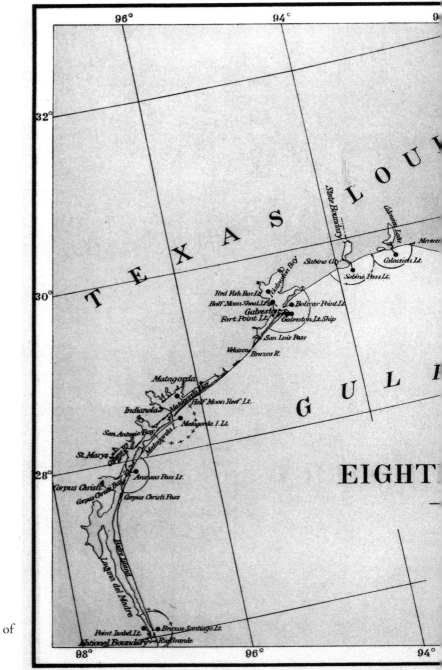

Map of Eighth Light-House District from 1881 Annual Report of the Light-House Board.

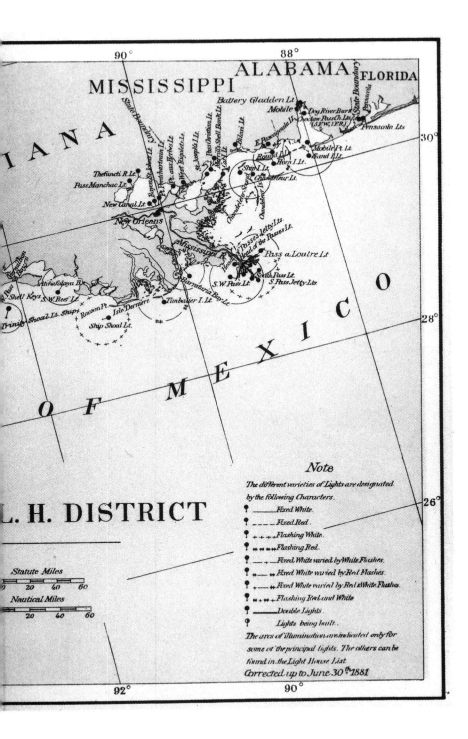

MISSISSIPPI ALABAMA FLORIDA

Battery Gladden Lt.
Mobile
Dog River Bar Lt.
Choctaw Pass Ch. Lts.
(5EW, 1ER)
Pensacola Lts

State Boundary
Pensacola

MISSISSIPPI

State Boundary Louisiana

IANA

E. Pascagoula Lt.
Pass Christian Lt.
Merrills Shell Bank Lt.
Biloxi Lt.
Round I.
Mobile Pt. Lt.
Sand I. Lt.

Thefuncti R. Lt.
Pass Manchac Lt.
New Canal Lt.
New Orleans

Bayou St. Johns Lt.
Pt. Pontchartrain Lt.
Pt. aux Herbes Lt.
West Rigolets Lt.
St. Josephs Lt.
Ship I. Lt.
Horn I. Lt.
Chandeleur Lt.

Chandeleur Sound
Chandeleur I.

Passes Jetty Lts.
Head of the Passes Lts.

Mississippi R.
Head of the Passes
Pass a Loutre Lt.

Barataria Bay Lt.
S.W. Pass Lt.
N.E. Pass Lt.
S. Pass Jetty Lts.

Barataria Bay Lt.

Barataria Bay

Atchafalaya B.
S.W. Reef Lt.
Shell Keys
Racoon Pt.
Isle Derniere
Timbalier I. Lt.

Trinity Shoal Lt. Ship?
Ship Shoal Lt.

G U L F   O F   M E X I C O

30°

28°

26°

L. H. DISTRICT

Statute Miles
0   20   40   60

Nautical Miles
20   40   60

Note

The different varieties of Lights are designated
by the following Characters.

———— Fixed White.
- - - - Fixed Red.
+ + + Flashing White.
•• •• Flashing Red.
- + - + Fixed White varied by White Flashes.
+ — + Fixed White varied by Red Flashes.
+ — + + Fixed White varied by Red & White Flashes.
+ •• •• Flashing Red and White.
———— Double Lights.
  Lights being built.

The arcs of illumination are indicated only for
some of the principal lights. The others can be
found in the Light House List.
Corrected up to June 30th 1881.

90°   88°

92°   90°

Miranda Younghans, who kept the Biloxi Light Station from 1919 until 1929. Courtesy of Biloxi Public Library.

Perry Younghans succeeded Mary Reynolds as keeper of the Biloxi Light Station. Owner of a nearby brickyard that had been shelled and destroyed by Northern forces, he used political influence to obtain his appointment after the war. He was 28 years older than his wife[6] and died within the year. His wife Maria assumed her husband's duties and continued at her post until 1919, winning the highest approval from the inspectors for her services. The bare outlines of Maria's tenure can be gleaned from the annual reports of the Light-House Board. In 1866 the illuminating apparatus was changed to a fixed Fresnel lens of the 5th order, with Franklin lamps that burned lard oil. The light was visible 13 miles in clear weather.

MARY REYNOLDS, MARIA YOUNGHANS, AND MIRANDA YOUNGHANS

In 1876 the damaged brick wall was replaced by a heavy timber bulkhead. In 1877 the keeper's house was described as "so far decayed as to render it difficult to make any repairs." In 1880 the house was torn down and a new one built. In 1888 "a new fence was put up all around the premises, the wash-house and wood-shed were rebuilt, and various other repairs made." A storm that same year did such damage to the breakwater that it had to be rebuilt again.

An appointment as extended as Maria Younghans's should have left behind interesting memorabilia, but a few newspaper clippings provide all that we know of her half-century-long career. In the Biloxi and Gulfport *Daily Herald* of August 22, 1925, an obituary states that Maria Younghans

> in the winter of 1870 called her brother-in-law, and effected through him the rescue of a man being swept out to sea about daylight, clinging to an upturned boat; and during the 1916 storm, when the heavy glass in the lighthouse tower was broken by a large pelican being blown against it, she and her daughter, mindful of the especial need of the light on such a night, replaced the glass temporarily and made the 'light to shine' as before, unimpaired.

An 1893 edition of the New Orleans *Daily Picayune*, reporting on a hurricane, stated that "Mrs. (Maria) Younghans, the plucky woman who was in charge of the Biloxi light, kept a light going all through the storm, notwithstanding that there were several feet of water in the room where she lived." The Light-House Board reported that the storm again destroyed the breakwater, but repairs were not completed until 1895.

Subsequent annual reports mention construction of brick walks, stable, washhouse, picket fence, and chicken house. The size of the oil house was doubled, and "a 900-foot wharf with a gate landing platform, steps, and boat davits at the outer end was built." A boathouse on piles was added later at the outer end of the wharf. In 1906 the old cisterns were removed and municipal waterworks installed.

As Maria aged, her daughter Miranda acted as her assistant, taking over many of her duties, and assuming all of them when Maria retired.

Maria had a female assistant keeper, Edna Holley. The light was electrified in 1926, during Miranda's tenure. She retired in 1929.

The Biloxi and Gulfport *Daily Herald* carried Miranda's obituary on February 6, 1933, noting "her unfailing courtesy and dignity gave hundreds of casual visitors to the light house a beautiful memory of her, and a visit to the light house was always described with many references to Miss Younghans."

In the mid-twentieth century the Biloxi Light was automated and the tower deeded to the city, which maintains the light as a private aid to navigation. The keeper's quarters were destroyed by hurricane Camille in 1969.[7]

<hr />

[1] Mary J. Reynolds is referred to as "Maria" Reynolds in the Harrison County Census for 1860 where she is listed as age 35, the Biloxi Lighthouse Keeper, and born in Maryland.

[2] Series E, Volume 54, Pettus.

[3] This letter is included in an article entitled "Biloxi's Lady Lighthouse Keeper," by M. James Stevens in *The Journal of Mississippi History*, date unknown.

[4] National Archives, Record Group 365, Treasury Department Collection of Confederate Records, E78, Lighthouse Bureau Correspondence, Box 2, provided by Sandra Clunies.

[5] In a paper for the 1998 Conference on Women and the Civil War, Clunies indicates that Reynolds was paid by the Confederate Light-House Establishment for services April 1 through June 30, 1861, and that the light was extinguished in 1861. Clunies also uncovered records indicating that Hannah Ham was paid by the Confederacy to keep Point Isabel Light Station in 1861 (personal communication dated August 22, 1999).

[6] From headstones in the Biloxi Cemetery: Perry Younghans 1814-1867; Maria Younghans 1842-1925. Information supplied by Murella Powell of the Harrison County Library System.

[7] Much of the information in this chapter was supplied by the Curator of Historic Facilities, Tullis-Toledano Manor, Biloxi, who provided mimeographed descriptions of the Biloxi Light Station, as well as copies of two articles about women keepers at Biloxi Light Station by Kat Bergeron published in the *Sun/Herald*, April 1, 1984. Other clippings came from the Historical Collections of the Biloxi Public Library. Technical details came from the annual reports of the Light-House Board.

7. Lights on the West Coast

Because ships were still the prevalent form of transportation in the first half of the nineteenth century, California's maritime heritage is linked to the opening up of the Pacific coast. California's shoreline is, in many ways, very inhospitable. For the early settlers the most noticeable difference between the East Coast and the West Coast was the lack of natural harbors. The Pacific was plagued with fierce winter storms, but in the 1,810 miles between the Mexican and Canadian borders, only San Diego, San Francisco, and the Strait of Juan de Fuca provided natural harbors suitable for riding out very rough weather. The rocky, irregular coastline abounded with unmarked dangers—reefs, ledges, offshore rocks, islands, and spectacularly tall points of land jutting far out into the ocean. Navigation in many areas was hampered by frequent days of heavy fog, making fog signals as important as shore beacons.

Not until 1840, during the war with Mexico, did United States forces occupy California, and in 1848 the Treaty of Guadalupe Hidalgo ceded California to the United States. A naval base was immediately established in San Francisco Bay. The discovery of gold that same year led thousands of people to pour into the mines of the Sierra Nevada. The sea routes drew the heavy traffic in the first months of the Gold Rush, promoting competition to turn out the fleetest clipper ships to make the trip around the Horn of South America. After 1850 a thriving coastal trade in lumber increased maritime commerce.

The completion of the transcontinental railroad in 1869 ended California's isolation, but sailing ships were still the cheapest way to move bulk cargoes—competing as best they could with the rapidly developing steamship, which soon made possible trade across the Pacific. All these ships needed aids to navigation to guide them along the treacherous Pacific coast.

A large number of light stations, including substantial towers designed to hold Fresnel lenses, were constructed on the California coast between 1854 and 1910. The first lighthouses, designed in Washington and built in the 1850s, were typically cottage structures with a tower rising through the center of the keeper's quarters. Little thought was given at first to the particularities of California's landscapes. Because wood was plentiful and cheap, they were built of redwood.

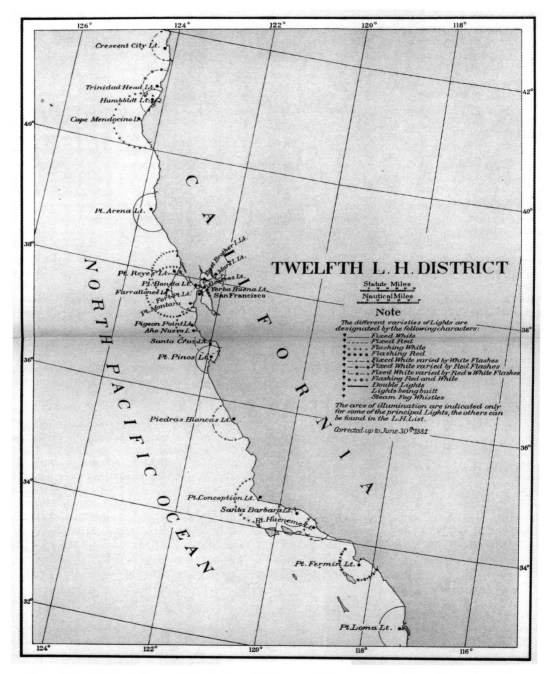

Map of Twelfth Light House District from 1881 Annual Report of the Light-House Board.

IX. Charlotte Layton, 1856-1860, and Emily Fish, 1893-1914, at Point Pinos Light Station, California; Juliet Nichols at Angel Island Light Station, California, 1902-1914

In 1855 Charles Layton, native of Oxfordshire, England, and veteran ordnance sergeant of a U.S. Army artillery regiment, became first keeper of Point Pinos Light at the entrance to Monterey Bay—the oldest continuously operating lighthouse on the West Coast. He brought his wife Charlotte (a native of Beaufort, North Carolina), three sons, and one daughter to the drab Cape Cod bungalow with the light tower in the center of its roof. That same year Layton was killed while serving as a member of a sheriff's posse chasing a notorious outlaw, causing the local collector of customs to write the Light-House Board in Washington, D.C., as follows:

> By this dispensation of providence, his widow, Charlotte A. Layton and four children have been left entirely destitute. I authorized her to continue at the post occupied by her late husband, and she is now discharging all the duties of principal keeper of the Lights at Point Pinos. I take much pleasure in recommending her for the place of principal keeper: she is a person eminently qualified for the position: she is industrious and bears an unblemished reputation.

Enclosed was a petition signed by a group of citizens in Monterey. "You will have the goodness," the collector of customs wrote, "to present the memorial to the Hon. Secretary of the Treasury and urge the confirmation of the appointment." The appointment followed promptly in 1856.

The lamp Charlotte tended burned whale oil, forced up from a tank by a gravity-operated piston. Its beam was concentrated by a third-order Fresnel lens manufactured in France. A falling-weight mechanism rotated a metal shutter around the light, causing the beam to be cut off to seaward 10 out of every 30 seconds. The weights were wound by hand. Title to the land on which the lighthouse stood was in dispute during Charlotte's entire tenure, and not settled until 1880.

Charlotte Layton was paid $1,000 a year, a salary much higher than those offered on the East Coast because the supply of labor in California lagged behind demand. Men outnumbered women 12 to one, but the men were largely attracted to the gold fields, giving women a wider range of employment opportunities. Charlotte had a male assistant keeper, George Harris, who earned $800. In 1860 Charlotte married Harris. Although the lighthouse service permitted a man to be in a subordinate role to a woman, Charlotte stepped down to again become assistant keeper. (In similar circumstances, Laura Blach, who was appointed keeper of the Ediz Hook Light Station at Port Angeles, Washington, in 1874, married the local customs collector. She,

This 1859 drawing of the Point Pinos Light Station in Pacific Grove, California, is based on an 1855 sketch by Major Hartman Bach. Courtesy of the National Archives, #26-LG-66-64.

CHARLOTTE LAYTON, EMILY FISH, AND JULIET NICHOLS

however, kept her keeper's position, earning $1,000 annually, with her husband becoming her assistant and earning $625 a year.)

After their retirement, the Harrises leased and ran the old Washington Hotel in Monterey. George Harris was listed in the 1870 census as a hotelkeeper. Charlotte died in 1896.

⊸✦⊶

Three decades after Charlotte Layton's tenure, the ambiance of Point Pinos Light Station was drastically changed. In 1893 widowed Emily Fish introduced to the modest Cape Cod bungalow a Chinese servant and furnishings seldom seen in a lighthouse—antique furniture, good paintings, fine china and old silver, leather-bound books. The servant, Que, had come with Emily from China when her husband gave up his consular post there. The furnishings came from the elegant house in Oakland where she and Dr. Melancthon Fish had lived after he established a private medical practice and began teaching at the University of California.

Emily was 50 when her husband died. Her naval officer son-in-law, who was Inspector of the 12th district of the lighthouse service, mentioned casually one day that the keeper of the Point Pinos Light was about to retire. Emily decided she would like the post, and her son-in-law arranged her appointment.

Point Pinos Light Station included 92 acres of sand and scrub. After transforming the keeper's house, Emily had topsoil brought in and spread so she and Que could plant trees, grass, and a cypress hedge around the yard. Then she added Thoroughbred horses to pull her carriage. Holstein cows grazed around the station, white leghorn chickens provided eggs, French poodles greeted visitors. As her mourning period ended, Emily rejoined the social life of the Monterey Peninsula, giving small dinner parties for artists and writers and naval officers from ships calling in Monterey Bay.

Authorized to employ laborers to help with the heavy work around the station, Emily listed in her log more than 30 male workers during

Following pages: *Entries from the official log for the month of April 1894, kept by Emily Fish at Point Pinos Light Station. Courtesy of the National Archives.*

1894 MONTH.	DAY.	RECORD OF IMPORTANT EVENTS AT THE STATION, BAD WEATHER, &c.
April	1	Wind Light — N. Clear —
	2	" " N. "
	3	" " N.N. "
	4	" " N. Hazy —
	5	" " N. Hazy —
	6	" N.N. Hazy — partly clear —
	7	" J. L. N. to S. Hazy — foggy morning —
	8	" Light N. Clear —
	9	" S.N. Clear —
	10	" fresh N. to S. Hazy — foggy morning
	11	" S.N. Clear — steamer bd north.
	12	" Light. N. " " bd. out south.
	13	" Light N. "
	14	" fresh N.N. Clear
	15	" Strong. N.N. Clear — partly cloudy
	16	" " N.N. Clear.
	17	" Light N.N. to S.N. Hazy — foggy night
	18	" " N.N. — "
	19	" " S.N. — "
	20	" " S.N. Foggy —
	21	" fresh. S. Cloudy — Shower —.05
	22	" S.N. Cloudy — Steamer passd South — 8.55 P.N. the night of the 21st on a sunken rock the Eureka going on her trip South afterward.
	23	" Light. S.N. Clear — Steamer passd. South
	24	" S.N. Cloudy — fresh at night
	25	" Variable S.E. Rain, & Hail, .12 —
	26	" fresh S.E. Rain in shower .35
	27	" fresh N. Rain showery .28
	28	" fresh N.N. Cloudy — clearing .
	29	" " Variable N.N. to S.E. Cloudy — fog at night
	30	" Light variable N.N. to S.E. Hazy —

Emily A. Fish Keeper —

Steamer b'd in & out South
Lumber schooner b'd in.
Steamer b'd in & out South.   Steamer from the north & out.
Steamer b'd in & out South. Labour D.S.S. Bivine came on duty to day.
Lumber schooner b'd out.

No vessels seen.

Keeper left the station at 6.a.M. on three days leave, having provided substitute
steamer passed north.
Returned to station at 6.30 P.M. everything in order —
Steamer b'd in & out South.
Steamer pass'd north.

Steamer pas'd.

Steamer d in & out South
very dark, no fog.
Steamer Eureka brought the survivors of the steamer Los Angeles which was wrecked at —
six miles below Point Sur. Passengers & crew were sent by rail to San Francisco.
Sailing vessel pass'd north.
Five bodies were brought to Monterey from Point Sur.   Coroners inquest
spoken verdict of manslaughter against 2d mate Reef Kogel —
Steamer b'd from north & out. Trucking schooner in tow of tug Fearless b'd in.
Steamer b'd in from the South. Trucking scow San Pedro in Tow tug Fearless—put back.
in port unable to face the weather. 27th Steamer pass'd South.
tug Fearless b'd out south & returned to port —
Steamer pass'd north.
Steamer b'd in & out South

her years as keeper—and stated that most of them were discharged for incompetence. Inspectors invariably noted that the Point Pinos Light Station was in excellent condition. In 1902 a tract of 52 acres lying between the light station and the sea was purchased so that stores and supplies could be landed from tenders.[1]

The inspector who had arranged Emily Fish's appointment had married her niece and stepdaughter Juliet, daughter of her sister, who was Dr. Fish's first wife and had died in childbirth in China. Emily had raised Juliet as her own child and had seen her married, at age 30, to Lt. Commander Henry E. Nichols. Commander Nichols, after his service as Lighthouse Inspector, was sent to the Philippines and died in 1898 during the Spanish-American War. As the wife of a former lighthouse service officer, Juliet was offered the post at the Angel Island Light and Fog Signal Station in San Francisco Bay in 1902. She tended a fog bell and an uncovered fifth-order lens with a fixed red light, which was moved by pulley out of the bell house each evening.

Emily Fish and Juliet Nichols were both on duty at their respective lighthouses early on the morning of April 18, 1906, to experience firsthand one of the world's most severe earthquakes. Emily was making her final rounds around 5 a.m. when she became aware of odd noises coming from the barn—the horses pounding the barn floor and the cows lowing uneasily. She went to the watch room to scan the landscape through the windows, trying to see what was disturbing the animals.

Emily wrote in her log that the first tremor of the "violent and continued earthquake" jarred the lighthouse at 5:13 a.m. The building shook and swayed, while cracking noises and tinkling sounds of breaking glass came from the tower. Outside the window, trees whipped and swayed.

The noises, the shaking of the earth, and the trembling of the building lasted for about two minutes. Emily and Que rushed up the stairs of the tower, noting as they climbed that a crack in the brickwork and coping of the tower was much enlarged. In the lantern the shock had bent a connecting tube and jarred the damper so that the lamp flame had run up much higher than it should. The violent tremors continued as they fought to control the flame.

CHARLOTTE LAYTON, EMILY FISH, AND JULIET NICHOLS

Emily A. Fish, who kept the Point Pinos Light in Pacific Grove, California, from 1893 to 1914. Courtesy of Monterey Public Library.

When the tremors finally ended, the two surveyed the whole station to assess the damage that had been done. The granite walls of the lighthouse had withstood the shocks, but the water in the woodhouse tank was thrown out on the floor. In the lantern, the prisms in the Fresnel lens had been jarred and had struck against each other, making the tinkling sound she had heard. When Emily attempted to report the damage to the district office in San Francisco, she found all telegraphic and telephone communication beyond Salinas, ten miles away, cut off. The train track was also obstructed, with no trains able to run.[2]

The 1906 *Annual Report of the Light-House Board* reported that "the damage was so great that it became necessary to tear down and rebuild the tower with reinforced concrete." In 1907 the repairs were completed.

The lantern and lens were removed for about 5 feet below the lantern floor. The original walls were of brick masonry 1 foot thick. The tower was rebuilt of reenforced concrete of the same thickness and general design. The reenforcing metal, consisting of 3/4-inch diameter rods laid vertically 8 inches apart, was set in holes drilled into the remaining walls; horizontal rings of 5/8-inch diameter wire cable were used to fasten the vertical rods. The station is supplied with water from the mains of the town of Pacific Grove. Minor repairs were made. A new 2-inch pipe, 2,200 feet long, was laid and connected with an elevated 4,000-gallon redwood tank. The tank is on the framed support and affords an efficient fire protection for the station.[3]

Juliet Nichols, at her post on Angel Island in San Francisco Bay on that fateful day in 1906, was making a final check of her equipment when she heard a rumbling sound. She looked across the water to the city silhouetted against the hills and was astonished to see buildings on the waterfront collapsing. Snatching her field glasses, she watched, horrified, as familiar landmarks crumbled into rapidly mounting piles of rubble. As the subterranean tremors continued, fires broke out, raging through factories, homes, and office buildings, until the skyline was blackened with smoke and ash.

Isolated on her island, Juliet watched the conflagration helplessly, trying to grasp the enormity of the tragedy unfolding before her eyes.

Fog bell ringing mechanism in Hooper Strait Lighthouse, Chesapeake Bay Maritime Museum, St. Michaels, Maryland. National Park Service photo by Candace Clifford.

Later she would learn that the earthquake had damaged every community within 100 miles of San Francisco.

Less than three months after that great disaster, Angel Island's fog signal broke down. According to the *Annual Report of the Light-House Board*, a new striking apparatus had been installed in 1905. Juliet was watching the fog roll in through the Golden Gate, as it so regularly does, and listening to the fog horns start up in lighthouses on both sides of the channel. She rushed to start her own equipment, only to have the machinery cough into silence a few minutes later. She could see the masts of a sailing vessel approaching above the fog. With no time for repairs, she snatched a hammer and began pounding the

In 2000, the 1855 Point Pinos Lighthouse continued as the oldest active aid to navigation on the West Coast. National Park Service photo by Candace Clifford.

bell, warning the ship away from her island. In her report on the malfunctioning of the equipment, she wrote that she pounded the bell at the prescribed intervals for twenty hours before the fog finally lifted.

Mechanical fog signals were notorious for breaking down. The mechanical pounding of the fog bell produced strong vibrations, which caused tension bars and hammer springs to break, even snapping the rope attached to the clockwork weight. The chapter entitled "Instructions for the Use and Management of Fog Signals" in *Instructions to Light-Keepers*[4] is one of the longest and most complex sections in the manual issued to light keepers.

CHARLOTTE LAYTON, EMILY FISH, AND JULIET NICHOLS

Two days later the Angel Island machinery failed again, forcing Juliet to repeat her exhausting ordeal. When the weather cleared, she summoned the lighthouse engineer to make repairs. Juliet Nichols's whole career at Angel Island was a battle with fog. Her log recorded periods of fog as long as 80 hours at a time and the many times she was forced to strike the bell by hand.

Why not, if a fog signal fails, just throw up your hands? Ships continued coming and going, fog or no fog, and the lighthouse keeper's duty was to prevent their wrecking themselves on the hazards along the shipping lanes. Angel Island was one of the worst hazards in San Francisco Bay, and Juliet Nichols took her duties very seriously. She richly deserved the commendations she earned for her dedication.

In 1914 both women retired. Emily Fish bought a house in Pacific Grove, where she lived quietly until her death at age 88 in 1931. Juliet lived equally privately in the hills of Oakland until her death in 1947. In the Pleasant Hill Cemetery in Oakland, the Fish/Nichols plot has two headstones bearing the names of Dr. M. W. Fish and Capt. Nichols, but nothing to indicate that two dedicated lighthouse keepers, Emily Fish and Juliet Nichols, lie there beside them.[5]

⌘

[1] 1902 *Annual Report of the Light-House Board.*

[2] This same story is told in "Emily Fish, the Socialite Keeper," by Clifford Gallant, *The Keeper's Log,* spring 1985, Vol. I, No. 3, p. 10.

[3] 1907 *Annual Report of the Light-House Board.*

[4] *Instructions to Light-Keepers: A photoreproduction of the 1902 edition of Instructions to Light-Keepers and Masters of Light-House Vessels,* pp. 33-50.

[5] Some of the information in this chapter is based on material collected by Clifford Gallant and incorporated in an article by him entitled "Emily Fish, the Socialite Keeper," in the spring 1985 issue of *The Keeper's Log*—the journal of the U.S. Lighthouse Society. Gallant's files, including private correspondence regarding Charlotte Layton, are at the U.S. Lighthouse Society headquarters in San Francisco. Ralph Shanks's two books contain further information.

Catherine Murdock, keeper of Rondout Creek Light on the Hudson River from 1867 to 1907. These woodcut illustrations appeared in the Kingston Daily Freeman *around 1888. Courtesy of the Rondout Lighthouse Collection, Hudson River Maritime Museum, Kingston, New York.*

X. CATHERINE A. MURDOCK AT RONDOUT CREEK LIGHT STATION, NEW YORK, 1857-1907

The first lighthouse at the entrance of Rondout Creek on the west side of the Hudson River was constructed of wood in 1837. George W. Murdock took his wife and two small children to that station in 1856, and found that the structure was already damaged by weather and ice. Although it was rickety and its safety questioned, Catherine Murdock was too preoccupied with producing a third child to give much thought to her surroundings.

Within a year after his appointment, George Murdock, who had gone ashore to purchase groceries, was found drowned—lying in the water beside his loaded boat, apparently on his way back to the lighthouse. Despite the tragedy and the attention her young children required, Catherine Murdock continued faithfully to maintain the light.

Others applied for her late husband's position, but local friends cited her diligence in her duties and recommended Mrs. Murdock for the post; she received the appointment in 1857. She spent a decade (including the Civil War years) in the old lighthouse, which was threatened repeatedly by severe storms and spring flooding. One storm in particular was so fierce that "the house rocked to and fro like a church steeple." Although Catherine feared the building might collapse, she knew how hazardous the river would be for boatmen without the light to keep them on course. She stayed at her post and kept the light shining in the tower.

In 1867 a new light station (often referred to as Rondout I) was constructed of bluestone on the south side of the creek entrance. The lantern was inside a square granite tower in the northeast angle of the dwelling on a round granite pier. The keeper's house was a solid, cozy structure with four rooms on each of its two floors; a local newspaper described it as "a little waterborne castle." Photographs of the time show the family parlor filled with dark Victorian furniture and the walls hung with framed photographs and prints.

Catherine Murdock lived more than 40 years in her castle. From her island home she witnessed the sinking of the passenger steamboat *Dean Richmond* and the burning of the steamboats *Thorn* and *Clifton* and the barge *Gilboa*. She told a newspaper reporter that the sight of the *Clifton* filled her with awe—one mighty mass of flame as it drifted in the current down the Hudson. She and her son rescued several seamen, nursing some back to health, but seldom reported these efforts because she disliked filling out the required paperwork.

One morning, before dikes were built on each side of the Rondout Creek entrance, Catherine's peaceful sewing was interrupted by a loud crash and the splintering of glass. She turned around and found a schooner's bowsprit sticking through the window and halfway into her room. The schooner had been crowded into the lighthouse by a steam tug towing a line of barges out of Rondout Creek.

Catherine found the lighthouse very pleasant in summer, when 20 or 30 visitors a day stopped by to climb the tower. But winters were cold and dreary, punctuated by "heavy and perilous storms." The worst experience that Mrs. Murdock recalled was a flood in December of 1878. On the previous day, as a very heavy snowstorm turned into pouring rain, a family friend visiting the lighthouse urged Catherine to go safely ashore. She replied, "I'm a woman, I know, but if the Lighthouse goes down tonight, I go with it."

When she climbed the tower at midnight to replace the lamps, all she could hear in the pitch dark night was the roar of rushing, rising water. At 3 a.m., the dam at Eddyville upstream on Rondout Creek gave way. The flood carried away houses and barns, tore boats, barges, and tugs from their moorings, and swept everything down the raging current. Catherine could hear the crashing in the darkness, but the lighthouse stood firm, the light shining brightly in the tower. When daylight revealed her surroundings, the flats were strewn with wrecks, and a schooner rested on top of the dike, with a live horse trembling beside it. The horse plunged into the water and swam a mile to shore.

In 1880 Catherine's son James was appointed assistant keeper. He and his wife lived in the lighthouse with his mother. Mrs. Murdock, who had remarried in the interim, retired in 1907 and moved ashore. James succeeded her as official keeper, remaining until 1915, when Rondout I was replaced with a three-story Rondout II, set on a concrete pier.

Rondout I was dismantled in the 1950s. Rondout II Light was automated in 1954, and the building was leased in 1984 to the Hudson River Maritime Museum, which periodically provides public access.[1]

⋘⋙

[1] This chapter is based on newspaper articles and a fact sheet supplied by the Hudson River Maritime Museum in Kingston, New York.

HARPER'S WEEKLY.

A JOURNAL OF CIVILIZATION.

Vol. XIII.—No. 657.] NEW YORK, SATURDAY, JULY 31, 1869. [SINGLE COPIES, TEN CENTS.
[$4.00 PER YEAR IN ADVANCE.

Entered according to Act of Congress, in the Year 1869, by Harper & Brothers, in the Clerk's Office of the District Court of the United States, for the Southern District of New York.

MISS IDA LEWIS, THE HEROINE OF NEWPORT.—PROF. BY MANCHESTER BROTHERS, PROVIDENCE, R. I.—[SEE PAGE 484.]

Ida Lewis, famous for her daring rescues at Lime Rock Light Station, was on the cover of Harper's Weekly *in July 1869. Courtesy of the U.S. Coast Guard Historian's Office.*

XI. IDA LEWIS AT LIME ROCK LIGHT STATION, RHODE ISLAND, 1857-1911

Idawalley Zorada Lewis, called Ida, was born in Newport, Rhode Island, in 1842.[1] Her father, Captain Hosea Lewis, was a coast pilot whose health was declining. In 1853 he became the first keeper of nearby Lime Rock beacon on a tiny island a third of a mile from the shore of Newport. At first there was only a temporary lantern and a rough shed that provided shelter when the keeper was on the island in bad weather. Lewis's family remained in the old part of Newport until 1857, when a Greek Revival building with a hip roof was constructed on the island. Lewis moved his family into the lighthouse when Ida, his eldest child, was 15.

A Newport journalist, George Brewerton, writing a feature story about Ida some years later, provides a detailed description of the lighthouse:

> The house itself is a square two-story building, plain even to ugliness, containing a parlor, dining-room and hall, with an L serving as a kitchen below. Above we find three bed-rooms, two large and one small, with a passage way and elevated closet, raised a step or two and reached by a door from the hall, to contain the lamp. Strangers imagine a tower, more or less lofty, . . . and are consequently disappointed . . . A narrow window, slightly projecting and fitted with glass upon three sides to hold the lamp, is all that the land-locked position of the place requires to fulfill the purpose for which it was erected. Within the bare walls the very humble attempts at furnishing speak of what the middle class might deem comfort, while the more affluent would regard it as indicative of a condition not very far removed from poverty itself.
>
> Ida's own particular sanctum is fitted with a cheaply finished cottage set, only remarkable as exhibiting a rude painting of a sinking wreck upon the head-board of her couch. . . . A sewing machine, a recent acquisition, with some little feminine nick-nacks,

complete the interior, while its two windows, one on either side, command a fine prospect of the harbor, looking toward the town.

Hosea Lewis had been at Lime Rock less than four months when he was stricken by a disabling stroke. Like many wives and daughters of lighthouse keepers before and after, Ida expanded her domestic duties, now increased by the care of her invalid father and a seriously ill sister, to include the care of the light—filling the lamp with oil at sundown and again at midnight, trimming the wick, polishing the carbon off the reflectors, extinguishing the light at dawn. All these responsibilities precluded further formal education for Ida.

Since Lime Rock was completely surrounded by water, the only way to reach the mainland was by boat. In the mid-nineteenth century it was highly unusual for a woman to handle a boat, but Ida, the oldest of four children, rowed her siblings to school every weekday and fetched needed supplies from the town. The wooden boat was heavy, but she became very skillful in handling it. (An article in *Harper's Weekly*, written after Ida had made several daring rescues, debated whether it was "feminine" for women to row boats, but concluded that none but a "donkey" would consider it "unfeminine" to save lives.) Ida was also reputed to be the best swimmer in all Newport.

In a newspaper clipping of the time, her father is quoted as saying,

> Again and again I have seen the children from this window as they were returning from school in some heavy blow, when Ida alone was with them, and old sailor that I am, I felt that I would not give a penny for their lives, so furious was the storm. . . . I have watched them till I could not bear to look any longer, expecting any moment to see them swamped, and the crew at the mercy of the waves, and then I have turned away and said to my wife, let me know if they get safe in, for I could not endure to see them perish and realize that we were powerless to save them.

Ida's skill at the oars was regularly tested. During her first year at Lime Rock, four young men who were out sailing nearly drowned. One of them had foolishly shimmied up the mast and rocked the boat to tease his companions. The boat capsized, and four boys who couldn't swim clung to the overturned hull, shouting for help.

Ida heard them and rowed to their rescue. In their terror, they almost dragged her overboard, but she pulled all four over the stern into her boat and returned them to land. This was only the first of a number of rescues that later made Ida famous.

Ida and her mother tended the Lime Rock Light for her father from 1857 until 1872, when he died. Her mother was appointed keeper until 1879, although Ida continued to do the keeper's work. Then Ida received the official appointment and her own salary ($500 a year). She continued at her post until her own death in 1911. On the night of her death the bells on all the vessels anchored in Newport Harbor were tolled in her memory.

Because of her many rescues, Ida Lewis became the best-known lighthouse keeper of her day. During her 54 years on Lime Rock, Ida is credited with saving 18 lives, although unofficial reports suggest the number may have been as high as 25. One such rescue, on March 29, 1869, is immortalized in a painting commissioned by the U.S. Coast Guard. The instructions to the artist noted that Ida Lewis's hair was dark brown and that she always wore a shawl over her shoulders and a "standard brown poplin dress." The instructions also urged the artist to "depict any rescue from the stern as Ida always brought the rescued person in from that location. Any other location

Lime Rock Light Station at Newport Harbor, Rhode Island, was kept by Ida Lewis from 1879 to 1911. The station now serves as a yacht club. Courtesy of the U.S. Coast Guard Historian's Office.

WOMEN WHO KEPT THE LIGHTS

Ida Lewis's daring 1869 rescue is immortalized in this painting commissioned by the U.S. Coast Guard. Courtesy of the National Archives, #26-B1-4.

would have capsized the boat." The artist was also told to "note the manner in which the oars are shipped," but instead has painted Ida extending one of her oars to the drowning man, while her younger brother Rudolph steadies the boat with his oar. The background of the painting includes a glimpse of the Lime Rock Lighthouse. The artist may have amalgamated details from several rescues into his painting.

Ida's fame spread quickly after the 1869 rescue, for a reporter was sent from the *New York Tribune* to record her deeds. Articles also appeared in *Harper's Weekly*, *Leslie's* magazine, and other leading newspapers. The Life Saving Benevolent Association of New York sent her a silver medal and a check for $100—a substantial sum to a young woman who then earned $600 a year. A parade was held in her honor in Newport on Independence Day, followed by the presentation of a sleek mahogany rowboat with red velvet cushions, gold braid around the gunwales, and gold-plated oarlocks. When she was 64, Ida became a life beneficiary of the Carnegie Hero Fund, receiving a monthly pension of $30.

George D. Brewerton, the Newport journalist, decided to write a pamphlet about her and went out to Lime Rock to seek her assistance. He described his visits in the flowery language of the time:

> In pursuit of this quest we have gone once and again, accompanied by our little boy, a juvenile greatly interested in Ida's dogs, rabbits and other Lime Rock pets, whose gambols served to amuse this lad while his father jotted down his notes at the table. Sitting in the snug kitchen of the light, with Ida in her favorite chair, the old invalid father occupying his corner by the stove, and her mother, with the bright face of Ida's younger sister Hatty, a girl of seventeen, flitting in and out to make up and complete, with the occasional presence of a sailor brother, the family. . . .

> And then when our work for the day was done Ida would man her ordinary boat, not the new *Rescue* presented to her by the people of Newport, with its elaboration of paint, carpet, and gilding, but the familiar old friend in which she won her fame, like herself at once plain, common-sense and reliable. Then with the ready hand of the practiced rower she would ply her oars till we were safely landed at the bridge, when waving her farewell with a promise to "tell us more next time we came," she would retrace her billowy way, cleaving the waves with steady stroke, while the ribbons of her sailor hat flutter gaily in the breeze.

Tales of Ida Lewis's skill and courage spread so widely that both President Ulysses S. Grant (1867-1877) and Vice President Schuyler Colfax (cousin of Harriet Colfax, keeper of the Michigan City Light Station—subject of the next chapter) went to visit her in 1869. Colfax went out to the lighthouse to meet her, but there are two versions of Ida's meeting with President Grant. One says that as Grant landed on Lime Rock, he stepped into water and got his feet wet. "I have come to see Ida Lewis," he remarked, "and to see her I'd get wet up to my armpits if necessary." The other version states that Ida rowed to shore and was conducted to the President's carriage to meet him and his wife.

Fame brought countless other visitors to the island to stare at Ida. Her wheelchair-bound father entertained himself by counting their numbers—often a hundred a day; nine thousand in one summer alone. No wonder Ida helped Brewerton with his pamphlet, for it would relieve her of answering the endless repetitive questions. She also permitted him to paint her portrait and sell photographs of it for 50 cents apiece "throughout the Union." Ida also received numerous gifts, letters, and even proposals of marriage (some of them offering to supply references as to good character). Ida was distressed by all the attention and fended off her many unknown admirers as best she could. Although few details are known, she did marry a Captain William Wilson of Black Rock, Connecticut, in 1870, but they separated after two years.

In 1881 the *Annual Report of the U.S. Life-Saving Service* reported that the highest medal awarded by the Life Saving Service had been presented to Mrs. Ida Lewis-Wilson,

> who, under her maiden name of Ida Lewis, has won a national celebrity by her early rescues. The papers accompanying the application made in her case to the Department show that she has saved from drowning thirteen persons, and it is understood that the number is greater. The special instance upon which the medal was awarded, was her rescue, on February 4th [1881], of two soldiers belonging to the garrison of Fort Adams, near Newport, Rhode Island. These men were crossing on foot, at 5 o'clock in the afternoon, or near twilight, between the fort and Lime Rock light-house, of which Mrs. Lewis-Wilson is the keeper, and suddenly fell through the ice, which had become weak and rotten. Hearing their drowning cries, Mrs. Lewis-Wilson ran toward them from the light-house with a rope, and, in imminent danger of the soft and brittle ice giving way beneath her, and also of being dragged into the hole by the men, both of whom had hold of the line she had flung them, she succeeded in hauling first one, and then the other, out of the water. The first man she got out entirely unaided; her brother arrived and helped her with the second. The action on her part showed unquestionable nerve, presence of mind, and dashing courage. The ice was in a very dangerous condition, and only a short time afterward, two [other] men fell through and were drowned, while crossing in the night in the immediate neighborhood of the scene of the rescue. All the witnesses unite in

saying that the rescue was accomplished at the imminent risk of the rescuer's life.

Ida's last recorded rescue occurred when she was 63 years old. A close friend, rowing out to the lighthouse, stood up in her boat, lost her balance and fell overboard. Ida, with all the vigor of her past youth, launched a lifeboat and hauled the woman aboard. When asked where she found her strength and courage, she replied, "I don't know, I ain't particularly strong. The Lord Almighty gives it to me when I need it, that's all."

In 1924 the Rhode Island legislature officially changed the name of Lime Rock to Ida Lewis Rock. The lighthouse service changed the name of the Lime Rock Light Station to the Ida Lewis Rock Light Station—the only such honor ever paid to a keeper. In 1927 the Bureau of Lighthouses removed the lens from the lantern and placed an automated beacon on a skeleton tower in front of the lighthouse. This light continued in service until 1963, when it was deactivated by the Coast Guard. Later the Newport Yacht Club bought the lighthouse and obtained permission from the Coast Guard to put a light back in the old lantern and maintain it as a private aid to

Ida Lewis in the boat she rowed between Lime Rock and Newport, Rhode Island, and which she used to rescue several people in danger of drowning. Courtesy of the Newport Historical Society.

Ida Lewis, official keeper of Lime Rock Light in Newport, Rhode Island, from 1879 to 1911. Courtesy of the National Archives, #26-LG-69-60.

navigation. Although adaptively used by the yacht club (and renamed the Ida Lewis Yacht Club), the building is virtually unaltered from the time that Ida Lewis lived there.

In 1995 the Coast Guard launched the first of a series of new keeper-class 175-foot coastal buoy tenders and named it *Ida Lewis*.[2]

¹ This chapter stems from multiple sources: a long entry on Ida Lewis in *Notable American Women* (Belknap Press of Harvard University Press, 1971); articles in U.S. Coast Guard publications; a mimeographed monograph from Coast Guard files entitled "Historical Paintings Project: Ida Lewis, Keeper of Lime Rock Lighthouse and the Rescue of Two Men on 4 February 1881," by Dennis L. Noble; and clippings from several Rhode Island newspapers, currently filed in the Coast Guard Historian's Office in Washington, D.C.

² U.S. Department of Transportation *News*, CG 34-95.

8. Keepers' Logs

Paperwork increased significantly under the U.S. Light-House Board. Keepers were to submit monthly reports on the condition of the station and make explicit specifications for any needed repairs. A monthly report on the fog signal and absences from the station was also required. Expenditures of oil, etc., and salary vouchers were to be submitted quarterly. Property returns were submitted annually as well as receipts for extra supplies; the keeper's receipt for property on taking charge, receipts for delivery of supplies, shipwreck reports, and reports of any damage to station or apparatus and any unusual occurrence were made as necessary. The keepers were expected to keep a daily-expenditure book, a general-account book, and starting in 1872, a journal. This journal, or log, recorded the events of the day in one line written across two pages. "The visits of the Inspector or Engineer, or of the lampist or machinist, and an account of any work going on or delivery of stores must be noted; as also any item of interest occurring in the vicinity, such as the state of the weather, or other similar matter. The books must be kept in ink, with neatness, and must always be kept up to date."[1] A legal-size ledger with marbled cover was supplied to the keepers by the Light-House Board.

These tasks obviously required the ability to read and write. Although earlier keepers (both men and women) were expected to maintain simple accounts, educational qualifications were not a major factor in employment decisions. Keeping the light involved mostly manual labor.

Instructions for keeping the log were pasted on the inside of the front cover. [See replica on facing page, taken from the front of a log.] Many of the logs, including those kept by women, are now on file in the National Archives in Washington, D.C.

Keepers interpreted the instructions in different ways. Most of them recorded little more than the weather. Others included details about cleaning and repairing the station. Others identified every ship that passed, or every supply boat that arrived and how long it stayed. They often mentioned visitors to the station. Some included personal information, such as illness, times when the keeper was away from the station, whether school was held, Sunday church services and funerals. A few gave information about domestic animals (cows, chickens, and the like). Some keepers filled in a page of accounts at the end of each month.

[To be pasted in the front of the Journal]

Journal

(1) The events of the day must be written on the same line across both pages and as a general rule, if carefully written, one line will be sufficient for a day's entries. One line must be left blank between each two days. The entries for each month must commence on a new page and on each Sunday the name of the day shall be written in the column for the month, in front of its proper date.

(2) The following entries shall be made in the Journal, viz:

Visits of Inspector, Engineer, Lampist, Machinist or any authorized person; a general account of all work going on at the station by the keepers or others; delivery of supplies; any item of official interest occurring at the station or in its vicinity; any unusual condition of wind or weather with abnormal readings of barometer or thermometer (ordinary conditions of wind or weather with ordinary readings of barometer and thermometer shall be entered only in the Expenditure Book). Where no Watch Book is kept, the fact whether or not all station lights which should be visible from a station are lighted shall be entered in the Journal. A list of such lights shall be entered on the first page of the Journal and it will then be necessary only to state in the remarks for each day: "All lights visible" or "All lights except _____ visible."

(3) No personal opinions or remarks on family affairs or ordinary household work shall be entered in the Journal. All entries must be confined to the subjects enumerated above, the Keeper using his judgment as to what occurrences are of sufficient importance, or official interest to warrant an entry in the Journal.

(4) If visitors are frequently at the station, the entry should be made as follows, viz: "A number of visitors from _____ at station today." or "A party of visitors from _____ at station today." At outlying stations where visitors are infrequent, the names of the visitors or the more prominent ones of the party, if large, should be noted, as well as the place from which they come, etc. The names of all persons (whether officials, workmen or visitors) remaining over night at any station, must be entered at the beginning and end of their visit.

(5) The times of leaving and returning to station of all Keepers shall be entered in the Journal and in cases where there is but one keeper, the name of the person left in charge of the station must be entered.

(6) The keeper shall make a general inspection of his station, light and fog-signal every Saturday and enter this fact, with the condition of the station, light and fog signal in the Journal. If anything prevents the Keeper from making this inspection on Saturday, the fact must be entered in the Journal and the inspection made as soon as practicable and entered in the Journal under the date made.

All of them recorded disasters such as a long boat foundering, a ship going aground, a seaman drowning. A few added mishaps such as a cellar flooding or machinery breaking down. Some pasted newspaper clippings in their logs or inserted letters between the pages. Some keepers wrote their names at the top or bottom of every log page. Others never identified themselves in the log, making it difficult to ascertain who the keeper was or whether the keeper was male or female.

Sarah Fine, who kept St. Marks Light in Florida from 1904 to 1910, did not write her name on every page. Her handwriting and her name appear, however, on June 18, 1904, under the last half-page of her husband's entries, but without any explanation of what happened to him.

Some of the entries in logs kept by women are tantalizingly ambiguous. One mentions an "abusive asst. keeper, being under the influence of liquer [sic]," but doesn't tell us how she coped.

Among the many logs kept by women, that of Harriet Colfax, keeper of the Michigan City Light on Lake Michigan from 1861 to 1904, is one of the most

LIGHT-HOUSE ESTABLISHMENT.
Form 306.

JOURNAL of Light-Station at St. Marks Fla

190 4
MONTH. DAY. RECORD OF IMPORTANT EVENTS AT THE STATION, BAD WEATHER, ETC.

June
1 Light Southerly breeze
2 Light S breeze to S & E
3 Moderate E breeze in the morning Hazy
4 Calm in the morning Hazy dry
5 Moderate Southerly breeze
6 Fresh S breeze to S & E
7 Light S breeze in the morning Cloudy
8 Light S breeze in the morning Cloudy
9 Light S breeze in the morning Cloudy
10 Light S breeze in the morning Cloudy Hazy
11 Moderate S breeze to S & E & S E
12 Moderate variable winds
13 Fresh S E breeze to S & S W
14 Fresh S E breeze to S
Inspector Received 1st H. Inspector
15 Fresh S E breeze to S
16 Light variable winds & N E
Inspector 17 received 1st H. in Inspection
Light & to E breeze to S
18 Moderate variable Winds
19 Light S breeze to S. W. &
20 Light S breeze in the moring cloudy
21 Fresh S breeze S S W
23 Moderate S breeze to S W
24 Light Southerly breeze
25 Calm in the moring Hazy dry
26 Light variable Winds N E
27 Light S breeze to S W
28 Moderate E breeze in moring
29 Calm in the moring Hazy
30 Fresh breeze to S E

Mrs Sarah J Fine
Keeper

interesting. Her fine hand and excellent grammar are of a higher quality than those found in logs kept by most of the other women, indicating a better-than-average education in the 1830s, when Harriet would have been in school. The significant entries in her log over a 20-year period make her station and her work come alive.

❧

[1] U.S. Light-House Board, *Instruction to Employees of the Lighthouse Service* (Washington, D.C.: 1881); and Clifford, p. 186.

Pages from keeper's log at St. Marks Light Station, Florida. The top half written by Charles Fine; the bottom half by his wife, Sarah Fine, who kept the light and the log following her husband's death in June 1904. Courtesy of the National Archives.

A 1914 view of Michigan City Light Station at Michigan City, Indiana, kept by Harriet Colfax from 1861 until 1904. No longer supporting an active aid to navigation, the station house now serves as a museum. Courtesy of the National Archives, #26-LG-56-30.

XII. Harriet Colfax at Michigan City Light Station, Indiana, 1861-1904

The short coast of the state of Indiana along Lake Michigan has at Michigan City a historic light that guided Great Lakes mariners for more than a hundred years. Its history began in 1835, when the founder of Michigan City deeded to the United States government a tract of land running from the bend of Trail Creek to the lake for the express purpose of constructing a lighthouse.

The first light was hung on a tall post located slightly west of the present lighthouse. The first lighthouse was built in 1837—a keeper's dwelling with a 40-foot-high white-washed tower topped with a lantern to house the light. The first keeper was paid $350 a year. The second keeper, appointed in 1844, was a woman, Harriet C. Towner, about whom almost nothing is known. She served until some time in the 1850s.

As the shipping of grain and lumber increased, a brighter light was needed to guide the ships. In 1858 the U.S. government constructed a new lighthouse on the shore, using joliet stone for the foundation and Milwaukee brick for the superstructure. The 1858 date can still be seen on the south wall. On the north end of the lighthouse was the lantern, which housed a fixed light with a Fresnel lens of the fifth order, visible for 15 miles. Sperm oil was used as fuel in the early years, with a switch to lard oil when it was discovered to be cleaner, and finally to kerosene when it became cheaper than lard oil.

A Mr. Clarkson served as first keeper of the new light. He was replaced in 1861 by Miss Harriet Colfax.[1] In the nineteenth century, when aids to navigation were the responsibility of the Treasury Department, many lighthouse keepers were political appointees. Miss

Colfax's appointment may have been arranged by her cousin, Schuyler Colfax, who was then a member of Congress and later became Vice President when General U. S. Grant became President in 1869.

Harriet Colfax had been a teacher of voice and piano in her hometown, Ogdensburg, New York, but moved to Michigan City in the 1850s with her brother, who founded and published the *Transcript*, the only local newspaper for many years. Harriet worked as typesetter on the paper and taught music. There were rumors of a romance gone awry. Then Harriet formed a close friendship with Miss Ann C. Hartwell, also a native of Ogdensburg, who had moved to Indiana to teach school. The two spent the rest of their lives together.

When failing health led her brother to sell the *Transcript* and seek a healthier climate, Harriet stayed on in Michigan City. She was 37 when she took up the lighthouse keeper's appointment in 1861, at an initial salary of $350 a year. Critics of the political influence that won her appointment mentioned her petite size and seeming fragility, but Harriet performed her duties without fail for 43 years, retiring in 1904 at age 80 because of failing health. She died a year later, shortly after Ann Hartwell's death.

A few events of her first decade keeping the light station on the Lake Michigan shore can be gleaned from the annual reports of the Light-House Board. The 1868 report said that "the dwelling leaks badly where the tower joins the roof; eaves troughs and conductors are needed; the roof required repairs, and a cistern and new outbuildings are wanted." Repairs were made the next year.

Piers guarded both sides of the entrance to Michigan City Harbor. On November 20, 1871, a beacon light and elevated walk were installed on the east pier, which extended 1,500 feet into Lake Michigan. This light too had to be maintained by the keeper of the shore light.

A year later all keepers began keeping their journals. Harriet Colfax's log is in the National Archives. Her crisp record of her daily activities gives a very vivid picture of her life at the Michigan City Light Station.

August 12, 1872: Clear & Warm, with light E. Winds. U.S. Tender Haze came in about 5 a.m. with supplies for the St[ation] House. Commodore Murray, St. House Inspector, called at the St. House. Expressed himself satisfied with everything about the establishment.

August 16, 1872: This is the day on which the Comet was to strike the Earth and demolish all things terrestrial—but failed to come up to appointment. The elevated walk [on the east pier] was run into by a Vessel entering the harbor & considerably damaged. 5 [ship] arrivals.

Colfax reported damage to the elevated walkway several times a year. This walkway was a wooden structure raised to some height above the pier on metal struts, allowing a pedestrian to reach the end of the pier when stormy water swept over the pier. Many moments of real danger were associated with that walkway.

September 18, 1872: Cold day. Heavy N. W. gale towards night. The waves dashing over both Piers, very nearly carrying me with them into the lake.

Some vivid images can be drawn from this cryptic entry. Colfax probably did not wear trousers, nor did she have yellow slickers to keep her dry. She may have worn an oilskin coat over her long dress, but her heavy skirts must have dragged around her ankles as they got wet. Freezing weather made the footing slippery. In cold weather the lard oil to fuel the beacon had to be heated to keep it from solidifying. If she was delayed, waiting for high waves to pass and too much time elapsed in reaching the beacon, the oil congealed and would not ignite, forcing her to return to the station house and reheat it. The storms she described buffeted her with wild gusts of wind, flinging not only waves across the walkway, but also blinding sheets of spray and sleet. When her task was finally completed, her soaked clothes would have been hung to dry by the wood stove. She would have no hot shower to revive her.

Barely ten days later, *September 29: Wind blowing a westerly gale all day & still rising at 5 p.m. Four vessels entered while the gale was at its height & ran against the elevated walk, breaking it in again. Went to the beacon tonight with considerable risk of life.*

The next day she mentioned that "the sails of the vessels which entered in yesterday's storm were hanging in shreds, but no other injuries sustained." A month later (November 7) in another storm, a vessel went ashore east of the piers. The next day's entry: *The Sch[ooner] Scotland went to pieces and sank in the night. Gathered the particulars of the wreck & reported the same to Com. Murray at Detroit—St. H. Inspector. The Gale of yesterday continued unabated. 1 arrival.*

Storms and nasty weather characterized Lake Michigan as winter set in. *November 19, 1872: Terrible day. Wind blowing a northerly gale— snowing & drifting. Crossing good on the ice [of the frozen harbor]. Looks as tho' Winter was fairly upon us, & a few days at the farthest would close up navigation. The* City of Tawas *has made her last trip & will go into Winter quarters here. Other vessels reported in Chicago papers following suit—also a good many wrecks, with fearful loss of life.*

Similar entries continued until *December 8: A terrible Northwesterly gale & snow storm. Growing cold very rapidly. Ice driven back into the creek & uniting permanently for the Winter this time, to all appearances. 3 p.m.: Storm increasing—Snow swirling & drifting. The most terrific*

A later pier at Michigan City Light Station in rough weather. The light keeper walked out on this type of elevated walkway to light the beacon at the end. Courtesy of the National Archives, #26-LG-56-32.

gale & snow storm of the season. I exhibited the Lights to-night as I never close up in a storm, but it is probably for the last time this season.

December 13: Put the lamps, etc. away for the Winter, covered from dust & dampness. (In December of another year she wrote that this end-of-season ritual included cleaning and polishing the lamps, wrapping up the lens in cotton batting and kerosene, storing all the parts in the oil house, and washing the glass and painted surfaces in the lantern.)

During the months when the harbor was closed, Harriet Colfax recorded only the weather. Shipping resumed the following May, when a log entry mentioned that she had requested a 130-foot extension to the elevated walk to the beacon. She justified the need for the extension barely two weeks later. *May 28, 1873: A terrible hurricane to-night at about the time of lighting up [the beacon]. Narrowly escaped being swept into the lake.*

When summer weather made her post more attractive, her entries mention "large numbers of visitors [came from the town] to see the lamps." Ships entering the harbor brought visitors as well.

August 17, 1873: The Supply Vessel Haze *put in (as usual) a very unexpected appearance this morning about 7 o'clock. Commodore Murray, St. H. Inspector, Captain Davis of the St. H. Board & Col. Wilkins, U.S.A., were aboard & came up to the house. The Officers expressed themselves much pleased with the buildings, lanterns, light, apparatus, etc. 2 arrivals. Obtained Com. Murray's approval of the extension of the elevated walk up to the beach line & also of a plank walk extending from the St. H. to the pier.*

By August 26 the extension had been completed, the walk laid, and a new floor put in the kitchen. But the walk extension did not remove all the difficulties of keeping the beacon lighted. *October 28, 1873: Terrific westerly gale. The waves dashing high over both piers, & over my head when on my way down to light the beacon. October 31: Main light and Beacon both bewitched tonight, requiring my constant attention during the entire night.*

The fall of 1874 began inauspiciously: *September 9: Man lost overboard from Sch[oone]r.* Herald. In October the Light-House Board informed Harriet that the beacon was to be moved to the west pier, which extended 500 feet further into the lake than the east pier. This would require the keeper to cross the creek by boat, walk along the other side of the creek, ascend the elevated walkway, climb the beacon ladder, and light the light. Work on moving the elevated walk from the east to the west pier was interrupted by a northeasterly gale. The mechanical pile driver and engine supporting the work were carried away in the storm.

On October 20 Colfax petitioned the Light-House Board to give her an assistant to tend the beacon. On October 29 she wrote that, because the elevated walkway had been removed, a gale kept her from reaching the beacon in the morning to extinguish the light. Not until November 16 was the walk completed and the beacon moved, but mariners were not yet apprised of the change. *November 20: The Sch[oone]r. Rowens came ashore outside the W. pier this night in consequence of the removal of the Light—will be a wreck.*

Apparently Colfax's request for an assistant was granted. *November 23: The man in temporary charge of the Beacon Light was unable to reach it tonight—consequently the Light was not exhibited. Storm increasing in fury when the Sun went down.*

The next day part of the elevated walkway was carried away and the beacon again unlighted.

Harriet recorded these kinds of damaging storms every year. *December 5, 1885: Gale continues, with snow—cold. Elevated walk badly damaged & beacon light damaged and put out. The beacon cannot be repaired this fall. Telegraphed Inspector & afterwards wrote him & the Engineer. Telegram from Insp'tor to "hang a lantern out," which I did.*

The next night the beacon was carried away in the storm. The following two nights Harriet sent a man in a tug to light the beacon, for there was no other way to reach it. The next day she asked permission to use the tug the rest of the season. Two days later she was told to close the lights as soon as possible, which she did the following day. In March the Inspector made her re-explain the causes of the darkened beacon and the need for a tug to light it.

Harriet Colfax, keeper of the Michigan City Light Station in Michigan City, Indiana, from 1861 until 1904. Courtesy of the Old Lighthouse Museum, Michigan City Historical Society, Inc.

In March of 1886 the entire superstructure on the west pier was carried away by a storm. The beacon was not replaced by a temporary light until June. In October the temporary light and the beacon structure were both carried away and thrown up onto the beach.

Every month Harriet mentioned preparing a monthly report, four times a year a quarterly report, and every winter an annual report to send to the Light-House Board. She recorded her various leaves of absence once she had an assistant to care for the station. In 1876 she visited the Centennial Exposition in Philadelphia. In the summer of 1882 she visited friends in Terre Haute for two weeks, and spent the

Christmas holidays in Terre Haute and St. Louis. In 1885 she visited her brother in Wyandotte, Michigan; in 1886 spent the Christmas holiday with her sister. In 1887 she requested leave throughout the entire winter when the lights were closed.

Many of her entries had a simple domestic quality to them. In May of 1879 she noted that she had sewn rings on lantern curtains for the beacon. The curtains were hung around the lamps in the daytime to keep the sun from spontaneously combusting the oil. Repeated entries mention cleaning and polishing the lamps and shining the brass. Other notations give glimpses of life in the station house. She writes almost every year of painting the stairs and floors and having the station house and the oil house painted. (Normally keepers were required to do all such painting, but women were exempted from painting whole buildings.) The paint could not have been very durable because once she mentioned the rain washing off the black paint that had just been applied to the lantern.

Every spring much of the sand that had washed into the yard during the winter had to be removed and the yard graded. Twice Harriet wrote that soot in the wood stove chimney caught fire, "causing quite a fright." Each fall she received a check ($20 to $30) for wood to heat her house. The Light-House Board continued to pay for wood until 1882, when they informed Colfax that she would have to pay for her own thereafter.

This sounds petty, but the keeper's small salary was augmented by free housing and many staples (delivered periodically by lighthouse tender) on which to live. In 1882 the keeper's allowance included 200 pounds of pork, 100 pounds of beef, 50 pounds of sugar, 2 barrels of flour, 24 pounds of coffee, 10 gallons of beans, 4 gallons of vinegar, 2 barrels of potatoes, 50 pounds of rice, and 13 ounces of mustard and pepper. The large amount of vinegar may have been for cleaning the lens, but why no salt?

In August of 1882 Harriet had trouble with a leaking lamp reservoir, and requested that the Light-House Board lampist come to fix it. She was told to switch lamps until he arrived. That same year several entries pertain to attempts to sink a tube well and find a steady supply of water. Finally she was authorized to spend $15 having an ordinary well dug. One of the tantalizing entries refers to repairs to the water closet, and then to having the outside of the water closet and lattices painted. She was obviously describing an outhouse.

She wrote of seeing a mirage from the lantern, of a total eclipse of the moon, of a double rainbow, of hailstorms, of glorious displays of Northern Lights. She recorded the day President Garfield was shot, and that she draped the station house in mourning when he died in 1881, and again when President Grant and Vice President Hendricks

Letter from Harriet Colfax to the Lighthouse Inspector, dated November 31, 1900. Found inserted between the pages of the log she kept. Courtesy of the National Archives.

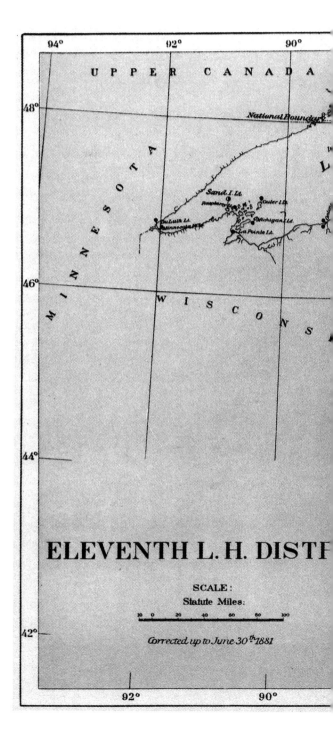

Map of Eleventh Light-House District from 1881 Annual Report of the Light-House Board.

HARRIET COLFAX

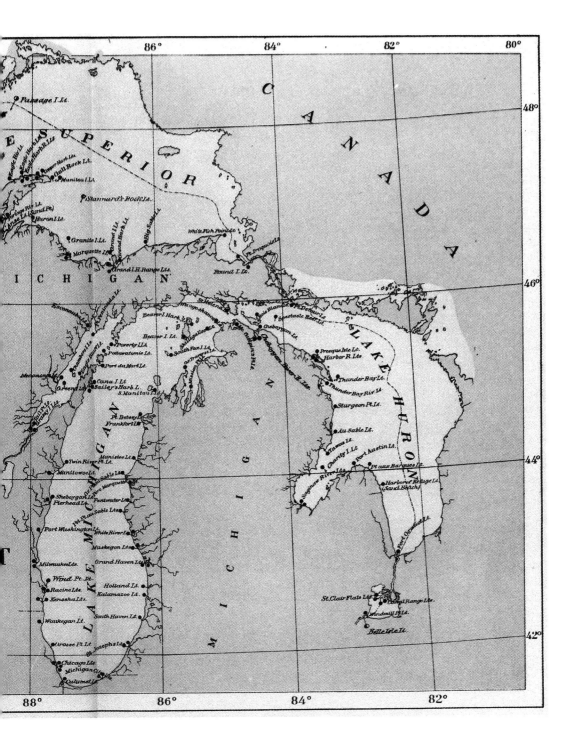

Passage I. Lt.

SUPERIOR

CANADA

Eagle Har. Lts.
Gull Rock Lt.
Manitou I. Lt.

Stannard's Rock Lt.

Granite I. Lt.
Marquette Lt.

White Fish Point Lt.

Round I. Lt.

ICHIGAN

Grand I. H. Range Lts.

Presque I. Lt.

MICHIGAN

Escanaba

Beaver I. Harb.

Beaver I. Lt.

St. Helena Lt.

Pt. De Tour Lt.

Bois Blanc Lt.
Spectacle Reef Lt.

LAKE HURON

Poverty I. Lt.
Pottawatomie Lt.

South Fox I. Lt.

Cheboygan Lt.

Presque Isle Lt.
Harbor R. Lts.

Menomonee
Green I. Lt.
Port du Mort Lt.
Cana I. Lt.
Bailey's Harb L.
S. Manitou I. Lt.

Thunder Bay Lt.
Thunder Bay Riv Lt.

Sturgeon Pt. Lt.

Pt. Betsey Lt.
Frankfort Lt.

Au Sable Lt.

Tawas Lt.
Charity I. Lt.

Port Austin Lt.
Pt. aux Barques Lt.

Manistee Lt.
Twin River Pt. Lt.
Manitowoc Lt.

MICHIGAN

Saginaw River Lts.

Harbor of Refuge Lt.
(Sand Beach)

Pte. Marquette
Sheboygan Lt.
Pierhead Lt.
Pentwater Lt.

Pt. St. au Sable Lts.

Port Washington Lt.
White River Lt.

Muskegon Lts.

Grand Haven Lts.

Milwaukee Lts.

Wind. Pt. Lt.
Racine Lts.
Kenosha Lt.

Holland Lt.
Kalamazoo Lt.

South Haven Lt.

Fort Gratiot Lt.

St. Clair Flats Lts.

Canal Range Lts.

Waukegan Lt.

LAKE MICHIGAN

Grosse Pt. Lt.
St. Joseph's Lt.

Windmill Pt. Lt.

Belle Isle Lt.

Chicago Lts.
Michigan City
Calumet Lt.

died in 1885. She mentions her confusion over an order from the Light-House Board outlining the official uniform she was supposed to wear (double-breasted coat with yellow buttons, dark blue trousers, and a cap bearing a yellow metal lighthouse badge). The inspector assured her that "women keepers were exempted" from this order.

Local deaths were recorded—the drowning of three fishermen after their boat capsized, a schooner captain struck by an engine, another drowned ten miles away from her light station. In 1885 the lighthouse keeper at Racine, Wisconsin, drowned in a storm. In 1886 a barge mate in her own harbor was struck in the head by a heavy log and killed.

Shipments of oil, wick, lamps, and other supplies were received and acknowledged. In 1882 instructions from the Station House Engineer told her to clean and polish all the lard oil lamps in preparation for exchanging them for kerosene (known as mineral oil) lamps. Occasionally she was asked to ship surplus oil to a neighboring light station.

One of the most surprising requests to come from the inspector was an instruction to "find out all about the birds and insects in this vicinity." Harriet noted that this was beyond her depth, so she "turned the letter over to the resident taxidurmist [sic]." A follow-up inquiry asked about bird migrations.

The Light-House Board must have been cramped for finances in 1882, for the assistant's position at the Michigan City Light Station was revoked. Harriet, then 58 years old, wrote letters all winter asking for help in tending the beacon. She kept both lights by herself through the following summer, and finally received permission in September to reemploy Mr. James, her former assistant. The following year he was demoted to the status of "laborer." In April 1885 a new assistant keeper, Mr. Timothy Fogarty, was appointed, but no explanation of the switch is given. In 1888 the Light-House Board reduced Miss Colfax's salary from $600 annually to $540. Again, no explanation is given, nor did Harriet record any judgments. If dealing with the lighthouse bureaucracy in Detroit gave her problems, she never indicated it. Her log entries were all factual and objectively phrased.

In 1892 the Light-House Board reported that "a number of persons have occupied the light-house grounds without authority. Measures have been taken to cause them to remove their shanties and other property." In 1894 an 83-foot-deep well was sunk, ending the fresh water problem. Every annual report for the rest of the decade recommended the addition of a fog signal to the station. Its construction was undertaken in 1904, and coincided with Miss Colfax's retirement.

Upon retirement, Harriet followed the last of the many instructions in *Instructions to Light-Keepers*:

> When a keeper resigns or is removed, a correct inventory of all public property under his charge must be made in the presence of his successor . . . No keeper who resigns or is removed, and no representative of such keeper, shall receive any balance on account of salary until he shall have accounted satisfactorily for all public property in his charge.[2]

October 6, 1904: Commenced taking inventory of public property. On October 8: Sold household effects preparatory to vacating dear old St. House. October 11: The new Keeper arrived today and made pleasant call at St. House. Miss Colfax's last entry in the official log was on October 12. She died five months later, at age 80.

The dwelling that continued to serve as the keeper's living quarters was remodeled in 1904, after Colfax's retirement, and enlarged by adding two rooms to each floor on the north side. This resulted in duplex apartments, the keeper and his family using all three floors on the east and the assistant keeper those on the west. The lantern along with its fifth-order Fresnel lens was moved from the house to the new fog signal lighthouse on the east pier at the entrance of Michigan City's harbor. In 1933 the light on the east pier was electrified. Three women—Abigail Coit, Julia Ebart, and Katy Reilly—served as assistant keepers in the years before the Coast Guard assumed responsibility for the Michigan City East Pierhead Light.

In the 1960s, the East Pierhead Light was automated and the City of Michigan City purchased the keeper's house and established a museum in it. A replica of the original lantern tower was placed on the roof in 1973.

¹ This chapter is based on Harriet Colfax's logs, archived in the National Archives in Suitland, Maryland; on clippings and information sheets supplied by the curator of the Old Lighthouse Museum, Michigan City Historical Society, Inc.; and on annual reports of the Light-House Board. Two articles about the Michigan City Light Station were also useful: "Michigan City: Indiana's Only Lighthouse," by Patricia Harris appeared in the spring 1987 issue of *The Keeper's Log*, U.S. Lighthouse Society. "A woman's place was in the lighthouse," by Susan Meyer appeared in the *USCG Commandant's Bulletin* 47-80.

² *Instructions to Light-Keepers* were issued several times by the Light-House Board. This quote is from page 12 of the 1902 publication.

XIII. Mary Ryan at Calumet Harbor Entrance Light Station, Indiana, 1873-1880

Temperament was a important ingredient in a successful lighthouse keeper, particularly in an isolated location. Not all women keepers reacted to their assignments with the equanimity of Harriet Colfax. Mary Ryan, who kept the Calumet Harbor Entrance Light in Indiana (located offshore on a pier) from 1873 to 1880 after her

Calumet Harbor Light Station on Lake Michigan just east of Chicago in 1914. This is the 1898 tower which replaced the 1875 wooden pierhead light. Courtesy of the National Archives, #26-LG-55-13.

husband died, expressed in her log her dislike of her post in no uncertain terms.

December 25, 1873: I was suppose [sic] to have been informed when this light would be discontinued [for the winter], not a vessel since the 15th of Nov. and nothing to light for and this is such a dreary place to be in all alone.

April 7, 1874: Oh, for a home in the sunny south, such a climate.

April 16: Such a time, everyone is despaired thinking that summer is never coming.

May 1: So cold, Mayday!, those people who go for flowers will be disappointed.

May 2: Nothing but gloom, without and WITHIN.

October 31: A promise of a cold hard winter as the signs show, so many out of employment at this early in the season, and what will it be before winter is over? God "only knows."

April 22, 1880: I think some changes will have to be made, this is not a fit place for anyone to live in.

July 31: This has been the most trying month of my keeping a lighthouse, the most important question, can anything worse come?

August 28: The lighthouse engineers never do anything for me.

August 30: Oh what a place.

November 1: This is all gloom and darkness.[216]

Mary Ryan was doubtless very pleased when her replacement arrived in 1880.

[1] These entries are taken from Mary Ryan's log, and were published in *The Keeper's Log*, U.S. Lighthouse Society, spring 1991.

XIV. JULIA WILLIAMS, 1865-1905, AND CAROLINE MORSE, 1905-1911, AT SANTA BARBARA LIGHT STATION, CALIFORNIA

The discovery of gold in California in 1848 led to rapid growth of ports on the Pacific coast. The Santa Barbara channel was particularly hazardous for early mariners because ships must make a 90-degree turn to round the land's sharp thrust out to sea. The nine Santa Barbara Islands lie just to the south. Before the Santa Barbara Light Station was erected in 1856, the channel had been a graveyard for ships.

Johnson Williams, originally from Kennebec, Maine, took his family to California in 1850. In 1856 they traveled by horse and oxcart to Santa Barbara to occupy the barely completed lighthouse (built in the uniform Cape Cod style popular in the 1850s) before there was even a road from the town to the mesa on which it stood. Santa Barbara was so small in those days that Mrs. Williams could invite all 30 Americans in the town to a Christmas dinner at the lighthouse in 1857. This would have been a major social occasion for women whose contacts with other women and their families were limited by distance and cumbersome transportation.

A Williams baby was born in the lighthouse two months before the three lamps were first displayed in the lantern. In 1904 this child, named Bion, wrote an entertaining account of those early days, entitled "The Santa Barbara Light and its Keeper."

The isolation of the lighthouse in his childhood provided many challenges. Bion's father had another job in town, leaving his mother very much on her own. Women who went west in the mid-nineteenth century had to perform a multitude of domestic tasks. Fresh water was to be caught in a cistern, but rain seldom fell. Mrs. Williams saddled a horse, took the baby in her arms, and, followed by two little girls, rode a mile to a spring to bring home cans of water slung to the saddle. She gathered wood for her cook stove in the same manner. She did her own sewing and mending. Many years later her grandson remembered particularly the excellent fresh-baked bread Mrs. Williams gave him, and the masses of orange and yellow nasturtiums blooming in the lighthouse yard.

In the early days all supplies came to the few stores in nearby Santa Barbara in small sailing vessels, arriving every month or two. When something ran out, customers waited for the next ship. Without even a right of way to the light station until 1877, getting to town to fetch supplies was a challenge in itself. Mission Creek ran between

Santa Barbara Light Station in California was first lighted in 1856. Julia Williams was keeper from 1865 to 1905; Caroline Morse from 1905 to 1911. The lighthouse was demolished in the 1925 earthquake. Courtesy of the U.S. Coast Guard Historian's Office.

JULIA WILLIAMS AND CAROLINE MORSE

the light station and the town and had to be waded. On those rare occasions when rain flooded the creek, the crossing was perilous.

Through some misunderstanding, another keeper was sent to the light station in 1860, and the Williams family retreated to a recently acquired ranch nearby. The new keeper stayed only briefly, but Mr. Williams was tired of the monotony of lighthouse routine, and sent his hired man every night to light the lamp. In 1865 his wife agreed to tend the light at a salary of $750 a year. She had produced another baby in the interim, and bore two more in 1866 and 1869. Mr. Williams continued ranching until his death in 1882.

Gradually the countryside was changing, with farms being fenced off and houses built. The Williams's son Frank grew corn and beans on the surrounding land and became a prosperous farmer. His brother Albert grazed dairy cows. In 1868 the *Annual Report of the Light-House Board* stated that

> extensive repairs have been made at this station. In the cellar a new floor has been made of bricks laid on edge in cement, in place of the old floor, which, being composed of bricks laid flat in ordinary mortar, was flooded by heavy rains. A drain leading outside from the cellar has also been constructed. A brick chimney has been substituted for the stove-pipe which passed through the roof and was considered unsafe. The tower and chimneys, where they pass through the roof, have been repointed with cement mortar. A storm-house has been built over and in front of the kitchen door, to keep out the rain.

In 1880 mineral oil replaced lard oil in the lamps. In 1881 "the roadway leading from the reservation to the county road was improved and repaired"; in 1893 a 50-foot well sunk; in 1894 a "galvanized iron windmill was erected on a steel spider tower over the well dug last year." The station received a new fourth-order lens in 1898.

Julia Williams retired in 1905, at age 80. In 1911 a local newspaper printed the following obituary:

> Mrs. Julia F. Williams, who for forty years was keeper of the Santa Barbara lighthouse, died Friday night at the Cottage hospital where she had been a patient sufferer since her fall [which broke her hip] at the lighthouse six years ago.

"The Lighthouse Lady," a title won by years of faithful service, was known to every naval officer and coasting captain that crossed the Channel. She was identified with the pioneer history of this city, being the first American woman in the presidio of Santa Barbara, and her memory was a veritable mine of early events. Her life of faithful service made hers one of the most historic and picturesque careers of the Pacific coast.

. . . Mrs. Williams was . . . at the time of her retirement the oldest incumbent in the lighthouse service.

In the forty years of service she was never out of sight of the house after dark. Every night she climbed the three flights of stairs at sunset and lighted the lamp. Every night at midnight the lamp was trimmed or changed for a fresh one, and every morning as the sun touched the mountain tops the same hand extinguished the light and drew the curtain across the lens and went about her household duties.

There were no fog signals and only one keeper, but there was only one wreck and that occurred one beautiful moonlight night when the careless captain allowed his vessel *The Pride of the Sea*, laden with merchandise, to drift too near the shore and was unable to keep off the rocks. . . .[1]

Julia Williams was succeeded at the Santa Barbara Light Station by Caroline Morse, who was keeper from 1905 to 1911, but details of her tenure are not available. The lighthouse was demolished in the earthquake of 1925 and replaced with an acetylene-powered light on a wooden tower.

⌒⌒

[1] The librarian of the Santa Barbara Historical Society provided clippings about Julia Williams, as well as a copy of her son Bion's memoir and an interview with her grandson. An article about the Santa Barbara Light Station appeared in *The Keeper's Log*, U.S. Lighthouse Society, winter 1993.

Julia Williams, keeper of the Santa Barbara Light, 1865-1905. Courtesy of the Santa Barbara Historical Society.

Postcard from around 1900 of the reconstructed Sand Point Light Station at Escanaba, Michigan. Mary Terry kept this light from 1868 to 1886, when she died in a fire that destroyed the lighthouse. Courtesy of the Delta County Historical Society.

XV. Mary Terry at Sand Point Light Station, Michigan, 1868-1886

Mary Terry's husband John was appointed the first keeper of the new light station on Sand Point at Escanaba, Michigan, while it was still under construction.[1] The couple moved from St. Catherines, Ontario, Canada, to Escanaba in 1867. John died of consumption before the lighthouse was completed. The citizens of Escanaba recommended that his wife replace him. Local government officials strongly opposed the idea, but Mary received the official appointment in 1868 and began the operation of the new light.

She apparently met the challenge. The Escanaba *Iron Port* reported that "she was a very methodical woman, very careful in the discharge of her duties and very particular in the care of the property under her charge." Mrs. Terry maintained the light on Lake Michigan's cold and windy northern shore for almost 18 years, using a wood furnace to keep warm in winter. In March of 1886 the handyman who helped Mrs. Terry with maintenance noticed that the wood near the furnace was hot. When he called the keeper's attention to it, she replied that she expected to be burned out one day, but added that she slept with one eye open.

Her premonition materialized during the following night, when fire destroyed the lighthouse.

When the alarm was given, at about one o'clock, the flames had entire possession of the building and had broken through the roof, and nothing could be done either to save it or its contents. It was known that the keeper Mrs. Mary L. Terry, occupied the building, and as she was not seen or heard from, it was at once apprehended that she perished in the house, and when the subsidence of the fire and the coming of daylight made an examination of the ruins possible, these fears were changed to certainties by the discovery of her remains therein.

The Deputy Collector in Escanaba wrote on March 5 to the Light-House Board:

> The Light House at Escanaba last night was destroyed by fire, but saddest of all was the remains of Mrs. Capt. Terry . . . found in the ruins deeming it my duty to thus inform you of this event, Mrs. Terry being Keeper of said Light House. Trusting I have acted properly in this case . . .[2]

On March 6, 1886, the *Iron Port* reported,

> Justice Glaser and a coroner's jury . . . viewed the remains (mere fragments—a portion of the skull, a few bones, and a small portion of the viscera), which were then placed in charge of D. A. Oliver and an adjournment taken to give time for the collection of evidence. The furnace by which the house was heated was in bad order, and it is not impossible the fire originated there.

Those who knew Mary Terry had difficulty believing that someone so efficient could have died by accident or her own carelessness. The fact that her remains were found in the oilroom in the southwest corner of the lighthouse, and not in her bedroom on the northeast side of the house, led some to speculate that she was the victim of murder, robbery, and arson. At age 69 she was reputed to be a woman of means, who had several thousand dollars in a savings account and had purchased several valuable building lots in the city.

The verdict of the coroner's jury a week later "that Mrs. Terry came to her death from causes and by means to the jury unknown was," according to the March 13 issue of the *Iron Port*,

> the only one that could be rendered. There was and is a general feeling of suspicion, based on Mrs. Terry's known cool headedness, that she did not come to her end accidentally, and this feeling is strengthened by the fact that the south door was found open and that the lock was found with the bolt shot forward as though the door had been forced, not unlocked, but the theory of robbery does not find support in the fact that money, gold pieces, were found where they would have fallen from the cupboard, the place where she usually kept what she kept in the house, and that a bundle of papers, insurance policy, deeds, etc., charred throughout but preserving its form sufficiently to show what it had been, was also found.

The verdict, then, was the only one possible, and the truth of the affair can never be known. There may have been foul play, but there is no evidence to justify an assertion that there was; no circumstances that are not consistent with a theory of accidental death.

⤝⥱⤞

[1] This chapter is based on material supplied by the Delta County Historical Society in Escanaba, Michigan, including an article in *The Delta Historian* entitled "Two Women among Nine Sand Point Lighthouse Keepers," by Richard Stratton, and two clippings from 1886 issues of the Escanaba *Iron Port*. The Historical Society has restored the Sand Point Lighthouse—taken out of service in 1938—to its original appearance.

[2] National Archives, Record Group 26, Entry 36, "Letters Received by the Light-House Service, 1829-1900."

9. A Family Affair

Harriet Colfax at Michigan City Light (Chapter XII) and Kate McDougal at Mare Island Light (Chapter XIX) were unusual in that they had no prior connection to lighthouses when they were appointed keepers. They differed from the typical women keepers as well in being well educated and having influential sponsors to help them win their appointments.

Most of the women who were appointed to tend the lights were already acquainted with lighthouse routines, having learned their arduous duties by helping a father or husband with his work. *Instructions to Light-Keepers* stated specifically, "A light-house must never be left wholly unattended. Where there is a keeper and one or more assistants, either the keeper or one of the assistants must be present. If there is only one keeper, some competent member of his family, or other responsible person, must be at the station in his absence."[1] Teen-age children as well wives shared all the responsibilities for tending the light, often performing heroic acts in their father's or husband's absence. Families carried on the keeper's duties when he could no longer perform them.

Keepers were often responsible for tending minor lights, which took them away from their station. They were permitted to pursue other jobs, such as fishing or piloting ships into harbors or farming. Members of their families, including wives and daughters, learned to keep the lights burning when their men were away. When a male keeper fell ill or died, many of these women simply took over their husband's or father's duties, often receiving official appointments because there was no pension system to care for them. The fifth auditor of the Treasury Department, Stephen Pleasonton, responsible for the lighthouse service from 1820 to 1852, was comfortable with appointing women keepers, and felt that widows and daughters of keepers were particularly worthy candidates for their positions. In a letter to his superior, the Secretary of the Treasury Thomas Corwin, dated June 7, 1851, Pleasonton indicated his frustration over the frequent politically motivated keeper appointments, feeling that widows of deceased keepers were far better suited for succeeding their husbands than inexperienced political appointees:

> It must be apparent to all who reflect upon the subject, that I have had much inconvenience and difficulty to encounter from the frequent changes incidental to our form of government, in the light-house keepers, who for a time do not understand the management of their lamps, and consequently keep bad lights

and waste much oil. So necessary is it that the lights should be in the hands of experienced keepers, that I have, in order to effect that object as far as possible, recommended, on the death of a keeper, that his widow, if steady and respectable, should be appointed to succeed him; and in this way some thirty widows have been appointed.[2]

Regulations published after the establishment of the U.S. Light-House Board stated, however, that "Females and servants are not to be employed in the management of lights, except by the special authority of the Department."[3] Apparently many women were granted special authority, for the numbers of female head keepers continued to increase. The 1870s saw the largest number of official female keepers—49—at any time in lighthouse history.

Fannie Salter and her son feed turkeys on the lawn of Turkey Point Light Station at the head of the Chesapeake Bay. Lighthouse families often married into another lighthouse family. Three of the four female keepers at Turkey Point Light Station, Maryland, were related. This light was kept by women for a period of 86 years. Courtesy of U.S. Coast Guard Historian's Office.

A circular dated April 30, 1879, from Naval Secretary George Dewey, Cmdr., USN, to all lighthouse inspectors, included three copies of another amendment to the Light House Regulations, by which it is provided that

> at isolated stations where there are two or more keepers, no women or children will be allowed to reside, unless by special permission of the Light-House Board previously obtained. No women will be permitted to reside on a light-ship under any circumstances.

His instructions went on to say that

> a copy of the amendment should be pasted into each copy of the book in your office entitled Organization and Duties of the Light-House Board edition of 1871 to face the back page. The Board requests that you will give notice to the principal keeper of each station affected by this regulation that it is to go into effect on and after the 1st of July next, and that he may make his arrangements accordingly.[4]

Offshore stations generally had several assistant keepers so that the keepers could rotate their duties, allowing each keeper time ashore to spend with his family.

At the Concord Point Light Station in Havre de Grace, Maryland, a single family tended the light for several decades. The first keeper was a hero of the War of 1812 who had valiantly manned the last artillery battery opposing the British at Havre de Grace. The eighth keeper, Esther O'Neill (1863-78), was the wife of the first keeper's son John, who kept the light from 1861 to 1863.[5] Esther followed him in that post, having witnessed much action at the beginning of the Civil War

> when Union troops sent from Pennsylvania to defend Washington were attacked by Marylanders loyal to the southern cause. Unable to continue troop movements by railroad, the Union set up ferries from Havre de Grace, adjacent to the lighthouse. Two [of Esther's] sons served for the Union: one killed in battle in 1864, the other wounded, captured, imprisoned at Belle Isle and . . . Richmond, released after three months, and later succeeded his mother as lighthouse keeper.[6]

The ninth keeper, Esther's son Henry, was followed by his son Henry, who kept the light until it was automated in 1920.

There are also numerous instances of members of lighthouse families marrying into other lighthouse families. Abbie Burgess (Chapter VII) is only one example of a female keeper who married the son of the new keeper after her father was replaced at Matinicus Rock. Fannie Salter, keeper at Turkey Point Light Station in Maryland (Chapter XXIV), was related by marriage to the Brumfield and Crouch families, which had provided earlier female keepers at that light. Fannie's daughter married back into the Crouch family.

━━◦◦◦━━

[1] *Instructions to Light-Keepers: A photoreproduction of the 1902 edition of Instructions to Light-Keepers and Masters of Light-House Vessels* (Allen Park, Michigan: Great Lakes Lighthouse Keepers Association, 1989), p. 13.

[2] U.S. Light-House Establishment, *Compilation of Public Documents and Extracts from Reports and Papers Relating to Light-Houses, Light-Vessels, and Illuminating Apparatus, and to Beacons, Buoys, and Fog Signals, 1789 to 1871* (Washington, D.C.: Government Printing Office, 1871).

[3] U.S. Light-House Establishment, *Rules, Regulations, and General Instructions* (Washington: William A. Harris, Printer, 1858), p. 8, from National Archives, Record Group 287, Box T674; this same regulation was repeated in the regulations issued in 1871.

[4] National Archives, Record Group 26, Entry 83, "Orders Sent to Field Officials, October 1852 - February 1896."

[5] This genealogy appears in the brochure published by the Friends of the Concord Point Lighthouse, as well as several other sources. An article in a Baltimore newspaper by Henry O'Neill's niece, Catherine O'Neill Gunther, states, however, that Esther O'Neill was the second of John O'Neill's daughters rather than his daughter-in-law. This would make her Henry's sister.

Information gathered by volunteer historical organizations is often based on secondary sources, stemming from local legend as much as from archival records. The validity of data can be very hard to verify.

[6] Sandra MacLean Clunies, "Recognizing Women's Efforts 1861-1865," p. 2.

Stony Point Light Station on the Hudson River, kept by Nancy Rose from 1871 until 1904. The 1826 tower is now in a state park. Courtesy of the National Archives, #26-LG-17-1.

NANCY AND MELINDA ROSE

XVI. NANCY ROSE, 1871-1904, AND MELINDA ROSE, 1904-1905, AT STONY POINT LIGHT STATION, NEW YORK

Our picture of Nancy Rose comes from an article published in the *New York Tribune* on June 28, 1903, shortly before she was preparing to retire, and another article in *The World* on November 20, 1905, when her daughter Melinda Rose resigned.[1] Nancy's intention was to move from the lighthouse high above the Hudson River on the crest of Stony Point to a cottage being built just behind the railroad station in the village at the base of the mountain.

The first keeper at Stony Point was Robert Parkinson, Nancy Rose's uncle, appointed in 1825. According to the *Tribune*, Nancy's husband, Alexander Rose, became the second keeper in the spring of 1852. A few years later, while carrying timbers for the bell tower that the government was then constructing, he ruptured a blood vessel; he died a few weeks later. After his death his wife took over his duties, trimming the lights and keeping the fog bell going from one end of the year to the next, for the Hudson River is often open to navigation throughout the winter. The *Tribune* said that Nancy Rose had lived in the little six-room cottage on the height for 50 years, 47 of them as official keeper, with sole responsibility for the point's two beacon lights and fog bell. Thus her tenure as keeper would have started in 1856, although her name does not appear as official keeper in "Lighthouse Keepers and Assistants" until 1871.

The newspaper article was written when Nancy was 79 and still in fine health, but she indicated to the *Tribune* reporter that she no longer found lighthouse tending as satisfying as it had seemed to her when, as a young widow and the mother of six small children, she took up her husband's duties.

The light station on Stony Point was built in 1826 on the foundation of Stony Point Fort, the old walls having long since been filled in to become a terrace of grass and shrubs. The Rose family frequently found old bullets and grapeshot, rusty and soil-eaten, around the fort. A flagpole marked the spot where Mad Anthony Wayne, of Revolutionary War fame, was supposed to have fallen. Nancy Rose's great-grandfather, Jacob Parkinson, was wounded in the same battle.

From the little balcony around the lantern one could see for miles up and down the Hudson River. The rolling hills followed its course, blue and misty as they melted away to the horizon. The trim little cottage on the mountaintop was surrounded with climbing roses and old-fashioned shrubs. Nancy Rose kept the interior immaculate.

In bad weather the fog machinery had to be wound up every three and three-quarters hours, and the lighthouse lamps replenished every midnight. In 1880 the fog bell was removed from the lighthouse at the top of the hill to a spot nearer the water and farther away from the house, requiring the keeper to hike back and forth to the site whenever fog closed in. In 1902 a red lens lantern was placed on top of the bell tower near the water, again increasing the keeper's duties, for it had to be trimmed and tended nightly. Nancy Rose's salary remained the same throughout, however—$500 a year.

Rose never left the station without notifying the inspector of her intended absence. She recorded weather conditions every day, along with the time of lighting and extinguishing the lamps, and the disposal of every ounce of supplies and inch of wick. The lighthouse inspector came unheralded in his tender at uncertain intervals, bringing supplies and making routine inspections of the five hundred aids to navigation in his district. He went over the entire premises, even the garret, cellar, and barn, but no criticism of Nancy Rose's lighthouse was ever known to be recorded.

The *Tribune* reporter also found everything about Stony Point Light Station "exquisitely clean. A new coat of gray paint has just made the woodwork resplendent, and the copper floor of the light chamber is burnished like gold. There is even a great canvas hood, with which the huge refracting lenses are covered during the day to keep any speck of dust from the polished metal and glass."

Only two of Nancy's six children survived—Melinda and Alexander—both of whom lived with their mother. Boredom seems to have played some part in the family's decision to leave the light station. Stony Point provided little of the excitement described by some of the other women keepers at busier spots. "You must have had many interesting experiences?" Mrs. Rose was asked by the reporter.

"No," was the answer. "Nothing ever happens up here. One year is exactly like another, and except for the weather, nothing changes."

Alexander, Jr., who was at the time supervisor of the little village of Stony Point, was asked if he would like to tend the light after his mother gave up the appointment. His emphatic reply: "Not much. I'd rather pick huckleberries over the mountain for a living."

Melinda's reaction was much the same. "I can't remember anything that has ever happened, except once our cow died, and several times it's been bad years for the chickens. But even the one wreck wasn't really what you might call a wreck, for nobody was hurt, and it wasn't mother's fault anyhow, for both the lights were burning as brightly as ever."

The wreck that was the highlight of their sojourn at Stony Point occurred in 1901, between 1 and 2 a.m. on a windy, rainy March morning, when the *Poughkeepsie*, a Central Hudson Steamboat Company passenger ship, went aground. Mrs. Rose had just returned from her nightly visit to the lighthouse and was changing her storm-soaked clothes when a pounding on her door startled her. Outside forty or fifty persons, among them seven women, sought shelter from the storm. The Roses did what they could, building a roaring fire in the kitchen stove to dry shoes and garments and dispensing hot coffee until the next train to New York was due.

Some of the Roses' disenchantment with lighthouse keeping may have resulted from the creation of a state park on Stony Point. After it opened, the lighthouse grounds were overrun in summer months with picnickers and sightseers who wanted to tour the whole place, including the tower.

Official instructions about visitors at light stations were very specific:

> Keepers must be courteous and polite to all visitors and show them everything of interest about the station at such times as will not interfere with light-house duties. Keepers must not allow visitors to handle the apparatus or deface light-house property. Special care must be taken to prevent the scratching of names or initials on the glass of the lanterns or on the windows of the towers. The keeper on duty at the time is responsible for any injury or defacement to the buildings, lenses, lamps, glazing of the lantern and to any other light-house property under his charge, unless he can identify the parties who have done the injury, so as to make them accountable for it; and any such damage must be reported immediately to the inspector or engineer of the district, with the names of the person or persons, if they can be ascertained. No visitor should be admitted to the tower unless attended by a keeper, nor in the watch room or lantern between sunset and sunrise.[2]

Reaching the lantern in the Stony Point Lighthouse involved three sets of steep steps and unlocking doors and trapdoors. Nancy and her children may have found the repeated climbing of the stairs and the supervision of large numbers of park visitors trying.

Nancy Rose apparently never left the light station to live in her new house, for she died in 1904. Her daughter Melinda could not have been completely disenchanted with the Stony Point Station, for she applied to succeed her mother as keeper. Lighthouse keepers had been moved into the Civil Service in 1896. When told that she was too old (53) to qualify under the new rules, Melinda sought the help of her Congressman in having the age requirement waived so she could take the examination and establish her eligibility. She had been assisting her mother for years, and received at least two temporary appointments. Her official appointment is recorded in "Lighthouse Keepers and Assistants" in 1904, but in 1905 she submitted her resignation with the following comment: "I find the care and responsibility too great for one keeper to attend to two lights and one fog signal for the sum of $560 per annum."[3] She also mentioned the loneliness of Stony Point in the winter. Melinda was succeeded by a male keeper.

⊷∞⊶

[1] Clippings, a short memoir by Melinda Rose, and copies of the correspondence regarding her appointment were provided as well by Stony Point Battlefield personnel.

[2] *Instructions to Light-Keepers: A photoreproduction of the 1902 edition of Instructions to Light-Keepers and Masters of Light-House Vessels* (Allen Park, Michigan: Great Lakes Lighthouse Keepers Association, 1989), p. 5.

[3] *The World,* November 20, 1905.

Beaver Island Harbor Point Light Station at the north end of Lake Michigan, kept by Elizabeth Whitney Williams from 1872 to 1884. Only the tower currently remains standing. Courtesy of the National Archives, #26-LG-55-7A.

XVII. Elizabeth Williams at Beaver Island Harbor Point Light Station, Michigan, 1872-1884, and Little Traverse Light Station, Michigan, 1884-1913

Elizabeth Whitney, born on Mackinac Island, Michigan, in 1842, grew up on Beaver Island in Northern Lake Michigan. In 1869, some years after she married Clement Van Riper, he was appointed keeper of the Harbor Point Light on the northeast side of the tip of Beaver Island in Lake Michigan. Elizabeth was unusual in the ranks of women keepers in that she nourished many of her solitary hours by writing. Much of her book, *A Child of the Sea; and Life among the Mormons,* deals with her childhood spent near a Mormon settlement on Beaver Island, but the last 20 pages detail her life in two lighthouses on Lake Michigan.

In the spring of 1870 a large force of men came with material to build a new tower and repair the dwelling, adding a new brick kitchen. A new fourth order lens was placed in the new tower and the color of the light changed from white to red. These improvements were a great addition to the station from what it had been. My husband having now very poor health, I took charge of the care of the lamps, and the beautiful lens in the tower was my especial care. On stormy nights I watched the light that no accident might happen. We burned the lard oil, which needed great care, especially in cold weather, when the oil would congeal and fail to flow fast enough to the wicks. In long nights the lamps had to be trimmed twice each night, and sometimes oftener.[1]

Then in 1872 tragedy struck.

> One dark and stormy night we heard the flapping of sails and saw the lights flashing in the darkness. The ship was in distress. After a hard struggle she reached the harbor and was leaking so badly she sank. My husband in his efforts to assist them lost his life. He was drowned with a companion, the first mate of the schooner *Thomas Howland.* The bodies were never recovered.[2]

In a letter that Mrs. Van Riper wrote to the chairman of the Light-House Board on November 15, 1872, she relates that her husband lost his way on the way to Mackinaw, where he went to "procure the assistance . . . for a schooner which was badly leaking. He went in the company of the first mate of the vessel for he could not get anyone else to go with him . . . Their boat was found that afternoon near Cross Valley badly broken to pieces . . . My husband lost his life in trying to aid . . . sailors who were in trouble."[3]

In her book she continued the story:

> Life then seemed darker than the midnight storm that raged for three days upon the deep dark waters. I was weak from sorrow, but realized that though the life that was dearest to me had gone, yet there were others out in the dark and treacherous waters who needed the rays from the shining light of my tower. Nothing could rouse me but that thought, then all my life and energy was given to the work which now seemed was given me to do.

> The light-house was the only home I had and I was glad and willing to do my best in the service. My appointment came in a few weeks after, and since that time I have tried faithfully to perform my duty as a light keeper. At first I felt almost afraid to assume so great a responsibility, knowing it all required watchful care and strength, and many sleepless nights. I now felt a deeper interest in our sailors' lives than ever before, and I longed to do something for humanity's sake, as well as earn my living, having an aged mother dependent upon me for a home.[4]

Although her first husband, two brothers, and three nephews died at sea, Elizabeth's own words make it clear that she loved her work.

> From the first, the work had a fascination for me. I loved the water, having always been near it, and I loved to stand in the tower and watch the great rolling waves chasing and tumbling in upon the shore. It was hard to tell when it was loveliest. Whether in its quiet moods or in a raging foam.

ELIZABETH WILLIAMS

Elizabeth Williams kept two lights on Lake Michigan. Courtesy of Beaver Island Historical Society.

My three brothers were then sailing, and how glad I felt that their eyes might watch the bright rays of our light, shining out over the waste of waters on a dark stormy night. Many nights when a gale came on we could hear the flapping of sails and the captain shouting orders as the vessels passed our point into the harbor, seeking shelter from the storm. Sometimes we could count fifty and sixty vessels anchored in our harbor, reaching quite a distance outside the point, as there was not room for so many inside.[5]

Elizabeth kept the Beaver Island Harbor Point Light for 12 years. In 1875 she wrote the Light-House Superintendent as follows:

> I expect to be married sometime in September, and will it make any difference about me keeping the light? Those wise people here say of course I cannot have the light if I marry, but I really don't see why I could not keep as good a light then as now. I have kept it almost 3 years alone and I believe that I have the name among Mariners of keeping one of the best Lights on the Lakes. The people here think I have had it long enough. They have opposed me just as they always did my late husband. Of course I would like to continue in the Light . . .[6]

Elizabeth continued her duties after her second marriage in 1875 to Daniel Williams. In 1884 she requested a transfer to the new lighthouse on Little Traverse Bay, where she remained for 29 years and wrote her book. She gave few details of her career at Little Traverse Light Station, but the annual reports of the Light-House Board state that in 1887, a 45-foot well was sunk to provide fresh water; it was replaced in 1891 with connections to the city water mains for protection against fire. A fog signal was added in 1896, and a beacon on the breakwater in 1899.[7]

Little Traverse Light Station at the north end of Lake Michigan was kept by Elizabeth Whitney Williams from 1884 to 1913. The station was deactivated in 1963 and now serves as a private residence. Courtesy of Beaver Island Historical Society.

ELIZABETH WILLIAMS

In 1900 the Light-House Inspector wrote to the Light-House Board as follows:

> I respectfully recommend that the salary of Mrs. Daniel Williams, keeper of the light station at Little Traverse, Michigan, be increased from $500 to $560 per annum, to date from May 1, 1900.
>
> As this station has now a fog-bell and no assistant keeper, the salary recommended will be in keeping with that of similarly equipped stations in this district . . .[8]

The salary increase was authorized on May 9, 1900.

[1] Elizabeth Williams, *A Child of the Sea* (privately printed by Elizabeth Whitney Williams in 1905; reprinted in 1983 by the Beaver Island Historical Society), p. 213. A short biography of Elizabeth Williams was provided by the Michigan Women's Historical Center, p. 213.

[2] Ibid., pp. 214-215.

[3] National Archives, Record Group 26, Entry 36.

[4] Williams, pp. 214-215.

[5] Ibid.

[6] National Archives, Record Group 26, Entry 36.

[7] Annual reports of the Light-House Board.

[8] National Archives, Record Group 26, Entry 24.

10. Annie Bell Hobbs at Boon Island Light Station, Maine, 1876

Annie Bell Hobbs's father was keeper of the light on Boon Island, off the coast at Kittery, Maine. A lighthouse was first built on this low, flat island during the War of 1812. A new tower of granite, shaped conically, 123 feet high (the tallest such structure along the Maine coast), was constructed in 1855. The lantern was reached by a circular stairway inside the tower. Nearby was the keeper's house and a small frame boat shed.

Life on Boon Island was precarious, because the waves washed across the entire island during storms, forcing the keepers to take refuge in the tower. Inclement weather often made it impossible for supply ships to come alongside and tie up. When Annie Bell was about 14 years old, she described life on Boon Island in a short piece published in *Nursery*, a children's magazine of the time. Her simple prose conveys the isolation and loneliness she felt.

Boon Island, Me.   Jan. 1876

Out at sea, on a rock eight miles from the nearest point of land, and about nine miles east of the town of Kittery, is Boon Island, upon which I have been a prisoner, with the privilege of the yard, the past two years. . . .

I will give you a description of the place and its inhabitants. The island is made up of nothing but rocks, without one foot of ground for trees, shrubs, or grass. The broad Atlantic lies before and all around us. Now and then sails dot the wide expanse, reminding me that there is a world besides the little one I dwell in, all surrounded by water.

The inhabitants of this island consist of eight persons—just the number that entered the ark at the time of the flood. There are three men, the three keepers of the light, whose duties are to watch the light all night, to warn the sailors of danger. There are two families of us, and in my father's family are five members. There are but three children in all—my little brother Stephen Green, three years old; little Mamie White of the other family, a little girl of four years, and myself, Annie Bell Hobbs.

Our colony is so small, and the children so few, that the inhabitants have concluded not to build a schoolhouse. Consequently I have my father and mother for teachers. . . .

After school-hours, I turn my eyes and thoughts toward the mainland and think how I should like to be there, and enjoy some of those delightful sleigh-rides which I am deprived of while shut out here from the world.

Boon Island Light Station. Courtesy of the U.S. Coast Guard Historian's Office.

In the summer we have quite a number of visitors, who board at the beaches during the season. They come to see the lighthouse and all it contains; and we are very glad to show them all, though it is quite tiresome to go up into the light a number of times during the day, since it is one hundred and twenty-three feet from the rock on which it stands to the light.

Up there among the clouds, my father and the other keepers have to watch, night after night, through storms as well as pleasant weather, through summer and winter, the year round, from sunset to sunrise; so that the poor sailors may be warned off from danger.

Annie Bell Hobbs

Not long after Annie Bell sent her account to *Nursery*, the lighthouse service decided that Boon Island was too dangerous for wives and children. Fierce storms often made it impossible for the keepers to get to the mainland or for sailing vessels to bring supplies to Boon Island. The Boon Island lighthouse crew was thereafter restricted to men.[1]

~≫≪~

[1] Annie Bell Hobbs's article was reproduced in Robert Carse, *Keepers of the Lights*.

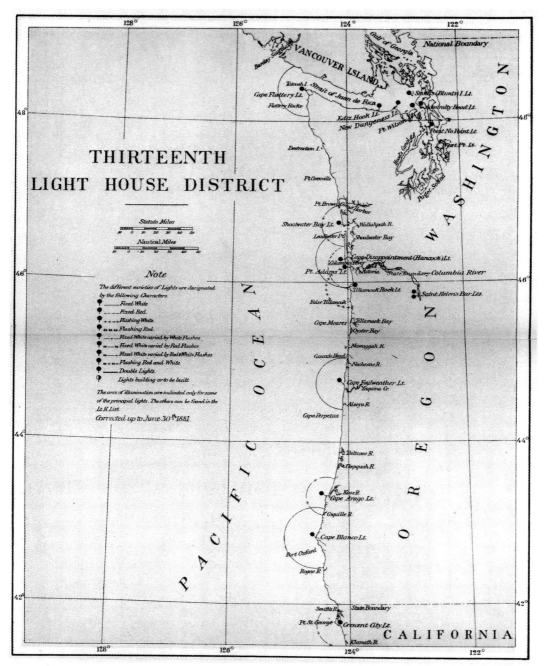

Map of the Thirteenth Light-House District from 1881 Annual Report of the Light-House Board.

XVIII. Mary Smith at Ediz Hook Light Station, Washington, 1870-1874, and Point Fermin Light Station, 1874-1882; Thelma Austin at Point Fermin Light Station, California, 1925-1941

Increased shipping into California's San Pedro Harbor led to the construction of a redwood-and-fir Victorian lighthouse on Point Fermin at the harbor entrance in 1874. The building design—Italianate with a square tower rising up through the keeper's dwelling—was identical to that of several other lighthouses erected in California at that time. Two large cisterns and the necessary outbuildings were included, with the entire station enclosed by a substantial fence. The lantern panes and the fourth-order Fresnel lens were shipped from France by way of Cape Horn. Lard oil was the first fuel, then kerosene, followed by electricity in 1925.

The first keepers were sisters, Mary and Ella[1] Smith, although only Mary is named as official keeper in 1874 in "Lighthouse Keepers and Assistants." Mary Smith had been keeper at Ediz Hook in Washington Territory 1870-1874, replacing her father, George Smith, when he resigned. It is possible that Mary's brother Victor Smith, having in 1860 secured a political appointment as a Special Treasury Agent, arranged his father's appointment as keeper at Ediz Hook, as well as assistant appointments for his sisters. Mary's appointment as keeper at Point Fermin (which paid $800 annually) and that of her

Mary Smith was keeper of Ediz Hook Light (shown here), Washington Territory, from 1870 to 1874 before receiving a transfer to the new Point Fermin Light Station in California. Courtesy U.S. Coast Guard Historian's Office.

sister as assistant keeper (which paid $600 annually) may have been arranged through Victor's influence in Washington.[2]

Genealogist Sandra Clunies writes,

Ella Smith resigned her position as assistant keeper at Point Fermin in January 1882, and her replacement was James Herald, who served but three months. Keeper Mary L. Smith was 'removed' in April 1882 and replaced by George N. Shaw, whose wife Carrie Shaw was briefly installed as assistant keeper, but at a greatly reduced salary of only $150. The assistant keeper position was abolished entirely in October 1882.[3]

The last keeper at Point Fermin was also a woman. Thelma Austin had gone to Point Fermin with her family in 1917, when her father was appointed keeper. When both parents died in 1925, Thelma, the eldest daughter, took charge of both the lighthouse and her brothers and sisters. Electrification of the light that year eliminated the endless routine of cleaning, polishing, and lighting lamps every evening and extinguishing them every morning. Thelma's duties were reduced to the flicking of a switch, permitting her to supplement her keeper's salary by working as a dental assistant in the daytime.

Thelma operated the light until two days before Pearl Harbor, when it was "blacked out." During World War II the lantern room was removed and replaced by a radar lookout. An automated light was established nearby after the war, leading the Coast Guard to turn the building over to a private preservation group. It has been restored to its earlier appearance and is today the popular centerpiece of a city park.[4]

Point Fermin Light Station in San Pedro, California, was kept by Mary and Ella Smith from 1874 to 1882 and by Thelma Austin from 1925 to 1941. Courtesy of the U.S. Coast Guard Historian's Office.

[1] We were under the impression that Mary's sister was named Helen until we received a brochure prepared by Sandra Clunies, entitled "1874-1882 Archives & Anecdotes; 1893 Vintage Photos: Point Fermin Lighthouse," prepared for the Harbor Lights Collectors Society, April 24, 1999.

[2] Ibid.

[3] Ibid.

[4] Based on an article in *The Keeper's Log,* winter 1987, by Lenore Nicholson, entitled "Point Fermin Lighthouse—Life Long Love Affair."

Point Fermin Light Station on the rugged California coast in 1893. Courtesy of the U.S. Coast Guard Historian's Office.

XIX. KATE McDOUGAL AT MARE ISLAND LIGHT STATION, CALIFORNIA, 1881-1916

Kate Coffee was born in 1842 in Florence, Alabama, daughter of a U.S. Army officer from an old Southern family.[1] She grew up in New Orleans. Her father's assignments took the family eventually to San Francisco, where Kate demonstrated her independence at an early age by marrying a Northern naval officer, Charles J. McDougal, in the year following the Civil War. The Northern and Southern in-laws always regarded each other somewhat warily.

Shortly after the birth of their first child, Captain McDougal and his sailing vessel *Jamestown* were ordered to carry to Alaska the papers authorizing the purchase of Alaska from Russia (1867). Kate didn't hesitate to accompany him, taking her baby daughter (also named Kate) to spend a year in Sitka.

Then Captain McDougal's ship was ordered around the Horn to Washington, so Kate and her toddler got on the train in San Francisco and crossed the country by rail, two months before the transcontinental railroad was completed (1869). (Presumably stage coaches carried passengers across the gap.) Her second daughter, Elizabeth, was born shortly after her arrival in Washington.

Kate's third child, Caroline, was born after they returned to Oakland. Captain McDougal was then ordered to the "China Station" in Japan. Kate took her three children across the Pacific on a paddle-wheel sailing vessel and spent a year in Yokohama. Her fourth child, Douglas, was born after her return to San Francisco.

Some time in the 1870s Commander McDougal was appointed Inspector of the 12th Lighthouse District, which comprised the

California coast. Among his duties was the inspection of lighthouses, the delivery of supplies from the lighthouse tender, and the paying of the keepers. In 1881 the lighthouse tender dinghy foundered as he and six others were landing through the heavy surf at the lighthouse at Cape Mendocino. Commander McDougal attempted to swim to shore, but currents carried him away and the heavy money belt he wore around his waist dragged him under the waves. Kate was widowed, with four children between the ages of 8 and 14 and a pension of $50 a month.

Although the Navy did not provide much money for widows in those days, it did try to take care of its own. Charles McDougal's father had been commandant of the Mare Island Naval Shipyard,

U. S. LIGHT-HOUSE ESTABLISHMENT.
1872.

LIGHT-HOUSE AT MARE ISLAND, CALIFORNIA.

Architect's rendering of the Mare Island Lighthouse in San Pablo Bay north of San Francisco, from the 1874 Annual Report of the Light-House Board, p. 85. Print courtesy of the U.S. Coast Guard Historian's Office.

KATE McDOUGAL

and relatives were still living there. Charles's Naval Academy classmate George Dewey (of later Spanish-American War fame) arranged for Kate's appointment as keeper of the lighthouse on Mare Island.

The Naval Shipyard sits at the north end of the island and was connected to San Francisco by a ferry. When the ferry ran aground, the pleas of the naval officers at the shipyard for better aids to navigation were heeded, and the Mare Island Light Station was constructed in 1873 near the point where the Napa River enters Carquinez Strait and flows into San Pablo Bay.

Photos of the Mare Island Lighthouse from this period show a two-story wooden building of the Italianate style used in several other California lighthouses, with the lantern housed in a square wooden tower. The building was perched on a high cliff, with a long flight of stairs down to the pier. Lighthouse tenders came to this pier every three or four months to leave supplies—oil for the light, food, and in

The Mare Island Light Station around 1900. The station no longer exists. Courtesy of Caroline Curtin.

the early days, fresh water. (A rain catch basin for a water system was not constructed until 1890—some years after Kate McDougal took up her post. In 1898 the lighthouse station was connected to the Naval Shipyard water supply.) Supplies were winched up the cliff in a wheeled cart on the rails located to the left of the stairs. A bathroom was installed in the house in 1892.

At the end of the pier was the fog bell, which the keeper activated whenever fog crept across the bay—a frequent and dangerous hazard to shipping. Beside the pier was a beach where Kate's children and grandchildren paddled about in the briny tidal water.

Because of their isolation, family members provided their own social life. Relatives from the Bay area came occasionally to make extended visits. Trips could be made by horse and buggy to the Naval Shipyard, but this took time and required some effort. Nor could the light ever be left unattended. It had to be lit every night of the year, and a constant watch kept day and night for approaching fog.

There was no school on the island, nor was it possible to travel daily from the lighthouse to the mainland. Kate McDougal educated her own children as best she could. Her third daughter, Caroline, did spend a year at a boarding school in San Francisco, but did not continue there. Few girls were educated to go on to college in the 1880s, but Kate's instruction was adequate to prepare her son for the Naval Academy, with some extra tutoring in math.

Kate's granddaughter remembers the base of the lantern tower in the Mare Island Lighthouse being lined with shelves of books, many of them gifts from friends and relatives who realized that Kate and the children needed reading material. All the Oz books were there, the Little Colonel series, and many sets of classics.

Kate and her eldest daughter loved flowers and planted a beautiful rose garden in front of the lighthouse. They probably also grew their own vegetables. Kate employed a laborer to do the heavy maintenance work, move the oil cart, and care for the cows. Someone constructed a two-room playhouse in the yard for the children, complete with glass windows, wooden floor, and even some cast-off furniture.

Kate McDougal, keeper of the Mare Island Light Station in California from 1881 to 1916, as a young woman. Courtesy of her granddaughter Caroline Curtin.

The officers at the Naval Shipyard who had known her husband kept track of Kate and assisted her when they could. During her first year on duty, these men put up poles and ran a telephone line from the shipyard to the lighthouse as a Christmas gift for her.

Kate was not a particularly enthusiastic housekeeper, much preferring her duties as light keeper to cooking and cleaning. A Chinese-American cook prepared most of the meals. Occasionally

Office of
CAPTAIN
OF THE YARD.

United States Navy Yard,

Mare Island, Cal. Jany 21. 1882.

Mrs Kate C. McDougal:-

My dear Madame -

Some two months ago many of your friends thought it would be pleasant to be able to wish you a "Merry Christmas" through a telephone, and to have you in closer communication with the inhabited centre of the Yard from that time on. So a christmas present of the telephone and its necessary outfit was determined upon.

Yesterday the work was completed, — a little late perhaps for christmas messages of 1881, but in good time for the many "Merry Christmas's" yet to come that we so heartily wish you.

In begging you to accept this token of our friendly and sincere appreciation, I am but acting as the mouth piece of those whose names appear below.

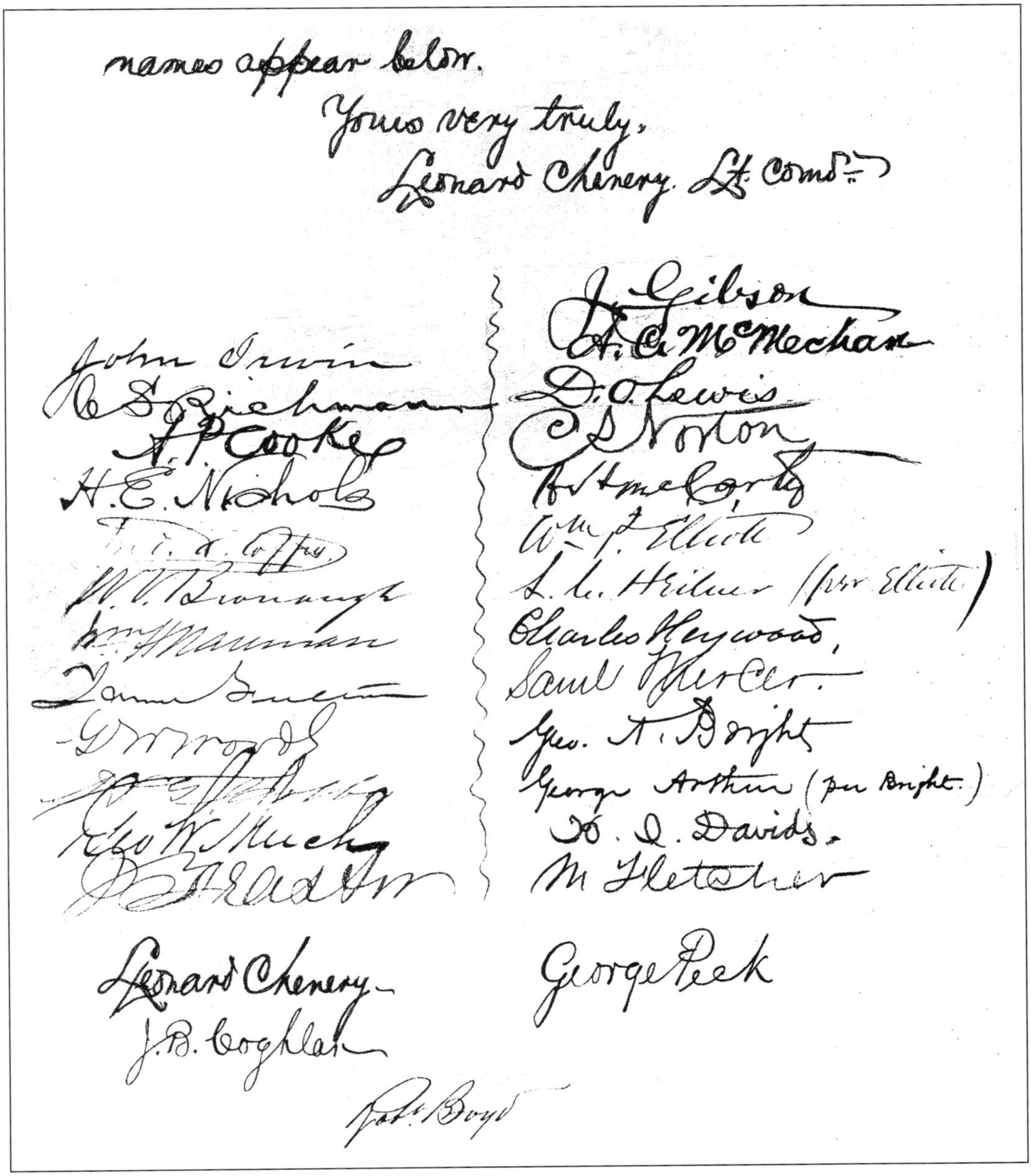

Yours very truly,

Leonard Chenery. Lt. Comdr.

John Irwin
C. S. Richman
F. P. Cooke
H. E. Nichols

Leonard Chenery
J. B. Coghlan

J. Gibson
H. A. McMechan
D. O. Lewis
C. D. Norton

George Peek

1882 letter from the officers of Mare Island Naval Shipyard to Kate McDougal at Mare Island Light Station. Courtesy of her granddaughter Caroline Curtin.

the wife of one of the ranks at the shipyard came to do housework, leaving Kate free to clean the lamps and chimneys, trim the wicks, fill the oil reservoirs, polish the brass and the prisms, and check the mechanisms that revolved around the lamp and rang the fog bell. Every night she opened the curtains in the lantern and lit the light. The last person who went to bed (whether mother, daughter, or granddaughter) was responsible for climbing into the tower to place a fresh lamp inside the lens.

Kate also wrote weekly, monthly, and annual reports, and spent a great deal of time making and recycling clothes for the children. Only the eldest daughter had new dresses. When she outgrew them, they were carefully taken apart, all pieces of material brushed clean and reversed, then reassembled for the next sister. Sometimes, if the material was still not too worn after use by three sisters, pants or jackets were made for brother Douglas.

Because no doctors or dentists were within easy reach, Kate patched and nursed her children as best she could. When her son decided to experiment with the effect of fire on dynamite, a piece of his ear was blown off. Kate retrieved the torn flesh and sewed it back on with a needle and black thread.

There was no church to attend. Daughter Caroline felt this lack, and as a young woman joined a group under the supervision of the chaplain at the Naval Shipyard in planning and raising funds to construct a chapel there.

Kate's eldest daughter married a naval officer. While he was away during the Spanish-American War, his wife and daughter returned to Mare Island to live in the lighthouse. The son-in-law stayed with them between assignments. This arrangement continued until Kate's retirement in 1916, so that one of her granddaughters grew up in Kate's lighthouse. Her son-in-law supplemented the education Kate and her daughter provided, based on his years of teaching English at the Naval Academy.

Kate's second daughter, "Bessie," distinguished herself in 1892 during an explosion at the shipyard. She was passing the naval hospital in her pony cart at the moment of the explosion. She promptly picked

Kate McDougal after her retirement as keeper of Mare Island Light Station in 1916. Courtesy of her granddaughter Caroline Curtin.

up the doctor who came dashing out and drove him to the magazine, where shells were still exploding. A watchman—half-dazed by a blow from a fragment and blinded with blood from a head wound—was stumbling from building to building, closing iron doors and shutters to prevent further disaster. Bessie stopped calmly to tie a bandage around his head, then gave assistance to other wounded until help came and she was ordered out of danger. Her bravery was recognized in an official tribute by the Secretary of the Navy.

After her two older sisters married, Kate's third daughter assumed many of the domestic duties in the household. Young Caroline learned at an early age to clean, do laundry, cook on the wood stove, care for and milk the cow, churn butter, groom the horse, and drive the buggy to the ferry to make trips to town for necessities.

In 1910 a new light (Carquinez Strait Lighthouse) was established across the mouth of the Napa River, eliminating the need for the Mare Island Light. It was abandoned in 1917, only nine days before the Navy Yard's ammunition depot exploded a second time, wrecking 13 buildings. The lighthouse survived, but was razed some time after 1930.

Kate retired in 1916 when an automatic fog signal was installed. All three of her daughters had married military men. Her son, in the Marine Corps, rose to the rank of Brigadier General. Her third daughter, Caroline, married to the medical officer at the Mare Island Naval Shipyard, was living with her family at the other end of the island. Kate went to live with them until her death in 1931.[2]

---

[1] This chapter is based on reminiscences by the late Caroline Curtin, Kate McDougal's granddaughter, born in 1909 at Mare Island Naval Shipyard while her grandmother was keeper of the lighthouse at the other end of Mare Island. Mrs. Curtin lived in Williamsburg, Virginia, and generously shared photos and memorabilia with the authors.

[2] A few technical details in this chapter were taken from annual reports of the Light-House Board. A chapter about Kate McDougal, based on personal recollections of another granddaughter, also appears in Ralph Shanks, *Guardians of the Golden Gate*.

XX. Laura Hecox at Santa Cruz Light Station, California, 1883-1917

Laura Hecox was born in 1854 in Santa Cruz, where her father owned two pieces of land.[1] At an early age she tagged after her father, exploring the tidal pools and sandy beaches along the northern edge of Monterey Bay, gathering shells and samples of rocks, minerals, and fossils. She was delighted when her father became keeper of the new Santa Cruz Light Station in 1869, permitting her to live on the very shore of her beloved bay. Some of Adna Hecox's ten children were already grown, but he taught the younger ones (Laura was the ninth) to help him tend the light.

Had Laura been born a hundred years later, she probably would have gone to college and become a marine biologist. Instead, by the time she reached her twenties, Laura was an amateur student of conchology, corresponding with other shell collectors and exchanging specimens. She also increasingly assumed the duties of caring for the light as her father aged and his health failed.

In 1883 Adna Hecox died. Laura was 29. Her brother-in-law, Captain Albert Brown, recommended to federal officials in San Francisco that Laura be appointed keeper because she knew the duties. Within a week the appointment was made with a salary of $750 a year. Laura lived on in the lighthouse for a total of 47 years. Three of her siblings were married there, and three members of the Hecox family died there. In later years one of Laura's brothers came back to live in the lighthouse, as did a sister and her husband. Laura took care of her mother until she died in 1908 at age 92.

The light station was an ideal post for a conscientious young woman whose avocation was collecting natural artifacts. In an 1896 booklet entitled *Beautiful Santa Cruz County*, Phil Francis writes, "The lighthouse is open to the inspection of the public three days in the week, and Miss Hecox not only exhibits to visitors the curious and costly mechanism of the great lamp, but takes pleasure in showing her own fine and interesting collection of marine curiosities. . . ."

The lamps in the Santa Cruz lantern were fueled before 1870 by high-quality lard oil, which was filtered from a half-gallon reservoir located up near the wick so that the heat would keep the oil fluid in cool weather. Lard oil was becoming very expensive—57 cents per gallon, compared to 8½ cents per gallon for kerosene. Santa Cruz Light was one of the first to be converted to the new fuel. An oil house to hold the very flammable liquid was not constructed until 1907. The tiny concrete structure (5 feet by 8 feet) was lined with wooden shelves that held 120 five-gallon cans—a year's supply.

The light was focused to a plane 67 feet above mean sea level by a fourth-order Fresnel lens, about one and one-half feet in diameter, with 18 levels of polished flint glass prisms. Laura kept the lamps, the lens, and the lighthouse in pristine condition. A writer visiting in

Santa Cruz Light Station at the north end of Monterey Bay in California was kept by Laura Hecox from 1883 to 1917. This station no longer exists. Courtesy of the National Archives, #26-LG-67-40.

☙✦

Laura Hecox, keeper of the Santa Cruz Light, collecting rock specimens. Courtesy of Santa Cruz City Museum of Natural History.

1904 described Miss Hecox as "a most pleasant little woman, standing guard at the front door, armed with a big feather duster." A dusty-looking visitor got a brisk whisking before being admitted inside, for Laura Hecox took *Instructions to Light-Keepers* very seriously:

> The utmost neatness of buildings and premises is demanded. Bedrooms, as well as other parts of the dwelling, must be neatly kept. Untidiness will be strongly reprehended, and its continuance will subject a keeper to dismissal. The premises must be kept clean and well whitewashed; grounds in order; all the inside painted work of the lanterns well washed, and, when required, retouched with paint. The spare articles embraced in the list of allowances must be kept on hand and examined frequently, and should be kept clean and in order for use.[2]

Since the six-room keeper's dwelling then housed only Laura and her elderly mother, one entire room could be devoted to Laura's private museum. She collected historical artifacts as well as biological specimens, and filled scrapbooks with clippings on taxidermy, architecture, literature, archeology, numismatics, philately, astronomy, religion, geology, botany, and California history.[3]

When a new public library was constructed in Santa Cruz in 1902, Laura Hecox was persuaded to donate her entire collection for permanent display. The Hecox Museum opened in 1905, and included exhibit cases devoted to dried starfish, crustaceans, Indian baskets and mortars, Eskimo artifacts, minerals, agates, gems, South Sea island curios, petrified woods, coral, shells, and turtle and tortoise carapaces.

After her mother's death, Laura remained in the small white keeper's house, faithfully tending the light, until her retirement in 1917 at age 63. She died two years later.

The historical record does not tell us whether Laura Hecox was frustrated by the limits of her education or career opportunities or tired by the endless daily routines of the lighthouse, or whether a young man ever came to call on her. But her love of nature made her an indefatigable collector. Laura formed a lasting connection with a museum, guaranteeing that we can still catch glimpses of her and the hobby that enlivened the 34 years she kept the Santa Cruz Light.

¹ The Registrar of the Santa Cruz City Museum of Natural History sent an article by Frank Perry entitled "California's Lighthousekeeper Naturalist." Laura Hecox's career is also outlined in Frank Perry, *Lighthouse Point: Reflections on Monterey Bay History.*

² *Instructions to Light-Keepers: A photoreproduction of the 1902 edition of Instructions to Light-Keepers and Masters of Light-House Vessels,* p. 6.

Laura Hecox and her mother on the porch of the Santa Cruz Lighthouse. Courtesy of the Santa Cruz City Museum of Natural History.

Robbins Reef Light Station on the west side of New York Upper Bay, marking shoal water on the New Jersey side of the main channel to the Manhattan docks. Kate Walker kept this light from 1894 to 1919. Courtesy of the U.S. Coast Guard Historian's Office.

KATE WALKER

XXI. Kate Walker at Robbins Reef Light Station, New York, 1894-1919

On the west side of the main channel into the inner harbor of New York City, a mile from Staten Island, is a hidden ridge of rocks that once caused numerous shipwrecks and great loss of life. In 1839 a lighthouse was built on Robbins Reef to guide large ships through Ambrose Channel. Because the ledge is submerged, a masonry island within a caisson was constructed on which to build the original tower.

In 1883 the Light-House Board replaced the old stone tower with a four-tier conical iron structure. The light in the 56-foot tower probably used kerosene to fuel the lamp inside a fourth-order Fresnel lens. The flashing mechanism consisted of eight large octagonal lenses set in a heavy frame that revolved between the stationary lantern and the outside windows; these lenses were rotated by a slowly descending weight at a rate that made the steady, diffused light flash brightly every six seconds as the focal point of one of the lenses came opposite the viewer. The light could be seen for 12 miles, except on foggy nights, and was one of the first lights the pilot of an incoming vessel saw when he entered Ambrose Channel. It showed him the way up through the Kill van Kull to Newark Bay, or on past the much brighter Statue of Liberty Light to the Port of New York.

The keeper's quarters fitted around the base of the tower like a donut. The kitchen and dining room were on the main floor. Lockers for clothes and closets for china fitted into the sides of the iron cone. Two bedrooms were on the smaller floor above.

The area of rock above water was hardly larger than the lighthouse itself and provided no mooring for boats. The keeper's skiff hung in davits from the platform. Access to the keeper's quarters was by a vertical metal ladder rising out of the water up to the kitchen door.

To assist mariners in identifying lighthouses in the nineteenth century, towers were painted in a distinctive combination of colors, which were listed in a *Light List* made available to any navigator by the lighthouse service. The Robbins Reef tower was painted white above and brown below—as it still is today.

The first keeper of the light in the iron tower built in 1883 was John Walker.[1] He had been assistant keeper at Sandy Hook Light Station. There in the boarding house where he ate his meals, he met a German immigrant woman waiting table. He decided to teach her English, married her, took her to Sandy Hook, and taught her to tend the light. John Walker's bride was in many ways typical of the working women who by 1870 made up one-quarter of all wage earners in the United States. They were either young single women or widows with children to support—many of them immigrants or children of immigrants. Seventy percent of them worked as domestic servants.[2] Kate was an immigrant with a fatherless child, who married a working-class man.

When John Walker received the keeper's appointment on Robbins Reef with a $600 annual salary, Kate was appointed his assistant at $350 a year. She told a visitor that her first reaction to the tiny foothold in the channel was to threaten to leave John Walker. "When I first came to Robbins Reef, the sight of water, which ever way I looked, made me lonesome. I refused to unpack my trunks at first, but gradually, a little at a time, I unpacked. After a while they were all unpacked and I stayed on."[3]

In 1886 John Walker, ill with pneumonia, was rowed to the mainland in the lighthouse dinghy by his young son. His last words to his wife were, "Mind the light, Kate." So she stayed and tended the light. When he died ten days later, a substitute was sent to permit Kate to arrange for his burial and attend his funeral, but she was back on the job before the day ended.[4]

Several men were offered Walker's post, but turned it down because Robbins Reef was too lonely. When Kate, then 40 years old with two children to care for, applied for the keeper's appointment, objections were raised because she was only four feet, 10 inches tall and weighed barely 100 pounds. Time proved that she was as good at her job as any man, for she not only kept the light burning, but rescued as many as 50 people by her own count—mostly fishermen whose boats were blown onto the reef by sudden storms. One such newsworthy incident was the wreck of a three-masted schooner that struck the reef and rolled over onto its side. Kate launched her dinghy and took aboard the five crew members, plus a small Scottie dog, whose survival pleased her enormously.

A *New York Times* reporter described Kate Walker in 1906:

> Mrs. Walker is a stolid, self-possessed, observant woman of the North German type, with shrewd gray eyes, hair that is still untouched by the tint of time, and a complexion as ruddy as a sea Captain's. She spends as much time on the terrace outside of her house as she does indoors, even when the wind blows and the salt spray compels her to don an oilskin jacket and a sou'wester. Seen from the decks of passing vessels, this terrace looks as though two goats walking side by side would be crowded. As a matter of fact, three persons arm in arm can promenade it very comfortably. In the good old Summer time, when this terrace is sheltered by an awning and dotted with tables and balcony chairs, it is a very inviting place.

> Mrs. Walker serves tea there when the bay is smooth enough for her friends to go out in rowboats to see her. In the Winter, when the water is rough and the lighthouse is surrounded with floating ice half the time, Mrs. Walker is virtually a hermit. But in Summer she is as "merry as they make 'em, . . ." She had a sewing machine and a wind-up phonograph, the latter for the benefit of her son and daughter, who get fidgety once in a while for the sound of a human voice.[5]

Once a year a lighthouse tender brought six tons of coal, a few barrels of oil, and a pay envelope to Mrs. Walker. Other than an occasional inspector's visit, she received little official attention unless the fog signal broke down. The *Times* article emphasized the limits of her horizons:

> All that she knows from personal experience of the great land to which she came as a girl immigrant from Germany is comprised within the limits of Staten Island, New York City, and Brooklyn.

She says she has never wanted to go West, South, or anywhere else. Hours of solitude have taught her, she says, that she is in pretty good company when she is by herself, and that happiness is being content with simple things. As a wife, mother, and widow, the happiest and saddest days of her peaceful life have been spent within the circular walls of her voluntary prison. She declares that if she were compelled to live anywhere else she would be the most miserable woman on earth, and that no mansion on Millionaires' Row could tempt her to leave of her own free will.[6]

Assisted by her son Jacob, Kate tended the Robbins Reef Light until her retirement in 1919 at age 73. Her only communication with the mainland was by rowboat or through the periodic calls of the lighthouse tender bringing supplies. "Lonely? Of course," she said in an interview in 1925. "But there are worse things than loneliness. Loneliness taught me that I could be a fairly entertaining companion for myself, and it made me realize that the simple joys of life are extremely satisfying."[7]

Every night Kate Walker trimmed the wicks while the lamps were burning and kept the reflectors clean and bright. In winter she removed frost from inside the glass windows, and during snowstorms climbed outside onto the balcony to clear the snow off the windows. The official instructions were: "To prevent the frosting of the plate glass of lanterns, put a small quantity of glycerin on a linen cloth and rub it over the inner surface of the glass. One application when the lamp is lighted and another at midnight will generally be found sufficient to keep the glass clear during the night."[8]

Mrs. Walker resented any implication that, because she was a lighthouse keeper, she had no household duties in common with other women.

> This lamp in the tower, it is more difficult to care for than a family of children. It need not be wound more than once in five hours, but I wind it every three hours so as to take no chances. In nineteen years that light has never disappointed sailors who have depended upon it. Every night I watch it until 12 o'clock. Then, if all is well, I go to bed, leaving my assistant [her son Jacob] in charge.

Jacob had come from Germany with his mother. One cannot help wondering if a fatherless child was the motivation for a young

Kate Walker, who kept Robbins Reef Light Station off Staten Island in New York Harbor from 1894 to 1919. Photo as it appeared in Harper's Weekly, *Volume 53, August 14, 1909. Courtesy of The Library of Virginia.*

girl to make that frightening voyage alone across the Atlantic to an unknown land. Kate and her husband John Walker had a daughter, Mamie, who boarded with a family on the mainland when it was time to go to school.

Jacob also spent much of his time ashore after his marriage. He was his mother's postman, marketman, and general courier. He also helped her land lumber that had washed away from railroad yards and shipyards along the shore—harpooning the logs with a rope and tying them to the railing until low tide, when they could be set up to dry.

Among other flotsam brought by the tide, Kate Walker hauled in a small box containing the body of a half-dressed baby, with its little hands stretched out as though appealing for help. Later in the morning she lowered the rowboat from the davits and took the lifeless body over to the coroner on Staten Island. Its identity was never determined.

The tide also brought occasional comedy to Robbins Reef, as a piece in *The New York Times* attested:

> It is a very swift and treacherous tide around there at times, fully as bad as at Hell Gate. A young man who took his sweetheart out in a rowboat from New Brighton one Summer Sunday afternoon did not heed the warning given to him. The tide carried him squarely onto the rocks around the lighthouse. His boat had a hole in her bow and was almost full of water when he assisted his companion up the iron ladder and let her have her cry out, while he conferred with the keeper. She dried their clothes while they sat out in the sun in decidedly castaway costume. Jake was ashore as night came on. He might not be back before morning. The girl was in despair.
>
> "We shall miss the last train to Fishkill," she exclaimed, "and I shall have to remain in town all night. Oh, what will they think of me?"
>
> "See here," said the young man. "You say the word and we'll get married on Staten Island tonight and send them a telegram explaining all about it."
>
> The girl was at first indignant, then reluctant, but finally consented. But how to get ashore? As luck would have it, one of Mamie's friends rowed out to the lighthouse that evening to pay a call. He entered into the spirit of the thing. The castaways were taken ashore, married by a minister at the close of the evening service, and started off on a happy honeymoon.[9]

When the light was obscured by fog, as it frequently was in winter, Kate went down into the deep basement and started the engine that

Robbins Reef Light Station, off Staten Island, was automated in 1966. Courtesy of the U.S. Coast Guard Historian's Office.

sent out siren blasts from a fog horn at intervals of three seconds. The siren made so much noise that she and her son didn't even try to sleep. Occasionally the fog horn machinery broke down. Then Mrs. Walker climbed to the top the tower and banged a huge bell. When the men at the lighthouse depot on Staten Island heard the bell, they knew they must visit Robbins Reef and make repairs as soon as wind and weather permitted.

In her years at Robbins Reef Kate Walker saw the progression from kerosene lamps to incandescent oil vapor lamps (similar to today's Coleman lantern) to electricity. The Light-House Board began experimenting with electric lights at the nearby Statue of Liberty and Sandy Hook East Beacon in the 1880s, and after 1900 it gradually converted those lighthouses that were near power lines.

The lighthouse historian Edward Rowe Snow, in his book entitled *Famous Lighthouses of America*, tells another story about Kate Walker— of a Christmas evening that turned into one of her most frightening experiences when a gale blew in:

> I knew that to the people coming through the Narrows the snow would hide the light. When I started the foghorn, the snow changed to sleet and drove against the windows. Then, above the driving of the sleet and the rattling of the wind, I heard a sound that I had heard but twice in twenty-five years and dreaded hearing.
>
> We kept our rowboat fastened to the outside walls by a chain, and if that chain broke, and the noise indicated that perhaps it had, I would be helpless to leave the tower.
>
> I wrapped myself up well and went outside. The wind nearly whirled me off the landing, while the sleet covered my hair like a hood. I felt my way along the icy walls. As I thought, one of the chains had been forced loose, and just then the loose end hit me in the eye. But I secured the boat and fought my way back toward the door.
>
> The gale blew in my face as I passed the iron ladder, and began to force me off the balcony. I knew that I could never get a foothold on the icy rungs of the ladder should the wind push me from the balcony. Finally I had to sink to my knees, and work my way to the door where I pushed it open, crawled inside, and shut and locked it. I knew my children would not attempt to return that evening, and so I spent Christmas that night alone in the lighthouse.

After her retirement at age 73 in 1919, Kate lived in a small frame cottage in Tompkinsville on Staten Island.[10] She died in 1931 at the age of 83. Her obituary in the *New York Evening Post* contained a moving passage:

A great city's water front is rich in romance. There is a strangeness about the restless ships that know the other side of the world; there are queer men busy in curious occupations; there are mysteries of sky and sea and weather. There are the queenly liners, the grim battle craft, the countless carriers of commerce that pass in endless procession. And amid all this and in sight of the city of towers and the torch of liberty lived this sturdy little woman, proud of her work and content in it, keeping her lamp alight and her windows clean, so that New York Harbor might be safe for ships that pass in the night.

Today, the Robbins Reef Light Station is automated, and the lighthouse is closed to the public. In 1996 the Coast Guard launched a buoy tender named in Kate's honor.[11]

⚓

[1] Much of the information in this chapter comes from a feature article in *The New York Times* on Sunday, March 5, 1906, Section 3, page 7, entitled, "Kept House Nineteen Years on Robbin's Reef." Other articles about Kate Walker appeared in *The Staten Island Historian* in 1978; in *American Magazine*, Volume 100, October 1925; and in *The Keeper's Log*, summer 1987, in an article by Clifford Gallant entitled "Mind the Light, Katie."

[2] See David Montgomery, *Beyond Equality: Labor and Radical Republicans 1862-1872* (New York: Vintage Books, 1967) for further information.

[3] *Philadelphia Ledger*, Sunday, August 23, 1925.

[4] According to U.S. Light-House Board records, John Walker died in 1890 not 1886 as stated in the feature articles about Kate. Kate was paid as a laborer to keep the light until receiving the keeper appointment on June 28, 1894. Her permanent appointment dates to July 7, 1895. Jacob received the assistant keeper appointment on July 27, 1896.

[5] Ibid.

[6] Ibid.

[7] Carol Bird, "The Loneliest Woman in the World," *Philadelphia Ledger*, August 23, 1925.

[8] *Instructions to Light-Keepers*, page 21.

[9] *The New York Times,* March 5, 1906.

[10] *Philadelphia Ledger*, August 23, 1925.

[11] U.S. Department of Transportation *News*, CG 21-96.

Port Pontchartrain Light Station on Lake Pontchartrain in Louisiana, kept by Ellen Wilson from 1882 to 1896 and Margaret Norvell from 1896 to 1924. Courtesy of the National Archives, #26-LG-37-51.

ELLEN WILSON AND MARGARET NORVELL

XXII. Ellen Wilson at Port Pontchartrain Light Station, Louisiana, 1882-1896; Margaret Norvell at Head of Passes Light Station, 1891-1896, Port Pontchartrain Light Station, 1896-1924, and New Canal Light Station, Louisiana, 1924-1932

A memo dated April 10, 1882, to the Chairman of the Light-House Board from the Light-House Inspector in New Orleans gave rather unusual reasons for nominating a woman keeper:

> Regarding the vacancy at Port Pontchartrain caused by the resignation of David F. Power, Keeper: I have requested the Collector of Customs, New Orleans, to nominate Mrs. Ellen Wilson to fill the vacancy, and he has kindly consented to do so.

> In explanation, I wish to say that Mrs. Wilson is a widow, with no resources except her own labor, and the mother of Mrs. Young, wife of the clerk in this office.

> Mr. Young, as is well known to the Board, has done efficient and faithful service here for over fifteen years, and I have requested the nomination of Mrs. Wilson in his interest.

> The circumstances are such that he can seldom get away from New Orleans, and this appointment, besides giving a support to a worthy woman who will perform the duty well, will afford him and his family a convenient place for recreation and a place of

refuge in case of epidemic. His services, I think, entitle him to some recognition, and I particularly desire that the appointment be made.[1]

Ellen Wilson kept the Port Pontchartrain Light from 1882 until 1896.

✦

Margaret Norvell carried on her husband Louis's duties as keeper of Head of Passes Light Station in Louisiana after he drowned in 1891, leaving her with two small children. She was appointed acting keeper there in 1891.[2] According to "Lighthouse Keepers and Assistants" in the National Archives, Margaret Norvell was appointed official keeper of the Port Pontchartrain Light Station on Lake Pontchartrain in Louisiana in 1896, following Ellen Wilson's tenure. A telegram to the Light-House Board in December of that year read as follows: "Mrs. Norvell has sold her cattle and packed ready for transfer to Port Pontchartrain and wishes to know if transfer as ordered is to stand to finish arrangements."[3] The response was positive.

The lighthouse was located near the east terminus of the Pontchartrain Railroad, where the town of Milneburg was a transshipment point and stopover for passengers on the way to and from the lake's north shore health resorts. The tower elevated the light 35 feet above sea level, making it visible for 10 miles. According to a *Times Picayune* article in 1934, Mrs. Norvell kept chickens and a Spitz dog in her yard, and a talking parrot in her kitchen. Her living room was lined with books and graced by a piano.

An account of "Madge" Norvell's career in the *Morning Tribune* of June 26, 1932, recounts the many lives she saved. "I have often rung my fogbell," she said, "to get help for overturned boats or to signal directions to yachts." During one storm, she threw a rope to the crews of both a yacht and a schooner, bringing them safely into the lighthouse and providing food and shelter for several days until the storm abated. On other occasions she rescued people from disabled sailboats and a small plane blown into the lake in a squall.

The article goes on:

It is not only the shipwrecked to whom Mrs. Norvell opened her doors. In every big hurricane or storm here since 1891, her lighthouse has been a refuge for fishermen and others whose homes have been swept away. In the . . . storm of 1903 Mrs. Norvell's lighthouse was the only building left standing on the lower coast, and over 200 survivors found a welcome and shelter in her home. After each storm she started the relief funds and helped the poor folk get back to normal.

This was a surprising career for a woman who came from a socially prominent New Orleans family and married a well-to-do cotton broker. His loss of his fortune led the Norvells into the lighthouse service, and Madge must have learned to love the lights. After her retirement she went every evening at sunset to the seawall to watch for the first flashing of the beacon she had tended. In her own words, "there isn't anything unusual in a woman keeping a light in her window to guide men folks home. I just happen to keep a bigger light than most women because I have got to see that so many men get safely home."[4]

The oil lamps at Port Pontchartrain were discontinued in 1929 and the tower turned over to the Orleans Parish Levee Board. Newspaper accounts of Margaret Norvell's death in 1934 indicated that she also tended the electrified light in the New Canal (West End) Light Station on Lake Pontchartrain from 1924 to 1932.

⌖

[1] National Archives, Record Group 26, Entry 24.

[2] National Archives, Record Group 26, Entry 82.

[3] National Archives, Record Group 26, Entry 24.

[4] Copies of the newspaper clippings cited above are filed among Clifford Gallant's papers at the U.S. Lighthouse Society in San Francisco.

11. Other Nineteenth-Century Women Keepers

A number of other intrepid women who kept lighthouses in the second half of the nineteenth century deserve their tribute. Many of their names appear in "Lighthouse Keepers and Assistants," but little other information about them has survived.

The Piney Point Light Station on the Potomac River in Maryland had four women keepers. Charlotte Suter served for an unknown number of years in the 1840s. Martha Nuthall was keeper there from 1850 to 1861. Eliza A. Wilson served there from 1873 to 1877, followed by Helen C. Tune from 1877 to 1883. Eliza Wilson carried out her husband's duties during his long illness and replaced him after his death in July 1873. In 1874, Congressman Wm. J. Albert received a complaint regarding nepotism in Mrs. Wilson's family, "I am informed she has a son holding an appointment in the Lighthouse Board. A son-in-law in the Treasury Dept. and also a daughter-in-law. . ."[1]

In 1853 Richard Edwards wrote the Light-House Board: "This is to inform you that my father the keeper of the Lighthouse at Point Look Out, St. Marys County, is no more. He died on the 14th inst., but the lights are strictly attended to and shall be until an appointment for the same is made by the executive." Only four days later the Secretary of the Treasury wrote revoking the appointment of Samuel Cullison as Keeper at Point Lookout in favor of Keeper Edwards's widow Martha.[2] Her daughter Pamela Edwards succeeded her, serving from 1855 to 1869.[3] Pamela watched events of the Civil War from her post. Genealogist Sandra Clunies writes, "The Union built the Hammond Hospital adjacent to the lighthouse, and then added an infamous prisoner-of-war camp, where nearly 4,000 Confederate soldiers died in a 16-month period. Letters suggest Pamela may have lodged female prisoners and female visitors at the lighthouse."[4]

Betsy Humphrey took over the light on Monhegan Island in Maine in 1862 when her husband died. At the time she had seven living children, one son having been killed in the Civil War and three daughters having died.[5] Several of the surviving children were old enough to be of considerable help to her. They would also have had neighbors on Monhegan Island, although it is some miles off the coast of Maine. Initially Betsy received the same salary as her husband—$820. In 1876 she was re-appointed at a reduced salary of $700 per year.[6] The salary reduction may have occurred because her duties tending the fog signal were

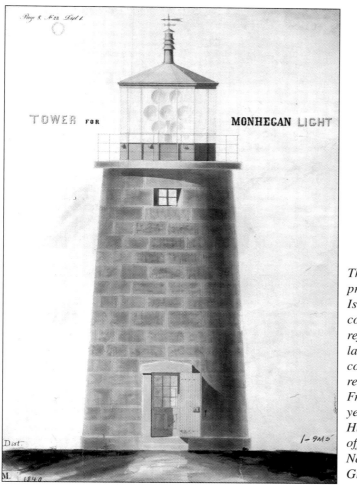

This 1849 drawing of the proposed Monhegan Island Lighthouse off the coast of Maine shows a reflector system in the lantern. The tower, completed in 1850, received a second-order Fresnel lens in 1856, six years before Betsy Humphrey became the official keeper. Courtesy National Archives, Record Group 26.

TOWER FOR   MONHEGAN LIGHT

eliminated when a first-class fog signal was installed on neighboring Manana Island.[7]

Interesting correspondence between the lighthouse inspector and the chairman of the Light-House Board in 1872 praises Mrs. Humphrey for "the assiduous care she takes of the interests committed to her charge."[8] A second letter relates to an unsatisfactory assistant keeper at Monhegan Island who failed to keep the fog signal in operation, "principally from laziness and ill-adaptation."[9] He was discharged and replaced. Betsy Humphrey remained at her post until her death in 1880.[10] Her third son Fred became assistant keeper that same year and served until 1901.

Julia Toby Brawn was an invaluable aide to her crippled husband Peter in tending the Bay City Light Station at the mouth of the Saginaw River in Michigan. They moved to the lighthouse, which was funded in those days by subscription from shipowners, in 1862. Peter Brawn died in 1873, and his wife tended the light until 1890, when her son became official keeper.[11]

An 1869 letter from the collector of customs in Milwaukee to the Chairman of the Light-House Board indicates an interesting change of heart:

> On the 8th inst. I had the honor to nominate Wm. G. Mallory for Keeper of the Light House at Sheboygan [Wisconsin] in place of L. Prazleton resigned. Since that time I have had strong recommendations from the citizens of Sheboygan . . . to nominate the wife of Louis Pape, a crippled soldier without arms or eyes. As the regulations of the Light-House Board forbid the employment of Females in Lighthouses without the consent of the Secretary of the Treasury, I respectfully ask permission to withhold the appointment of Wm. G. Mallory should it arrive and to nominate Mrs. Pape instead. I think she is qualified to discharge the duties of keeper . . .[12]

This is a reference to a Light-House Board policy requiring Board approval for the appointment of a women keeper. Eva Pape did receive her appointment, however, as did many other women.

Many widows of Civil War veterans received the sympathy of the Light-House Board. Caroline Litigot was nominated to replace her husband Barney as keeper of the Mamajuda Light on the Detroit River in Michigan, "She is worthy and needy, having a family of children to support, and left penniless by the death of her husband, whose decease was the result of wounds received in the U.S. Army during the war of the rebellion."[13] The Inspector, however, objected to her appointment, citing poor health and incompetence. George Howes was appointed on July 14, 1874, to replace Acting Keeper Litigot.

On July 24, 1874, an appeal from Senator Chandler to the Secretary of the Light-House Board requested that he

> . . . suspend action on the removal of Mrs. Litogot Keeper of the Light House at Mama Juda. . . The vessel men all say that she keeps a very excellent light, and I think it very hard to remove this woman, who is faithful and efficient, and throw her upon the world with her children entirely destitute when her husband lost his life in defense of the Union. . . her numerous friends and

OTHER NINETEENTH-CENTURY WOMEN KEEPERS

Caroline Litigot kept Michigan's Mamajuda Light from 1874-1885. Courtesy of the National Archives #26-LG-51-13

sympathizers, many whom are masters and pilots of vessels, competent to speak of the manner in which she has kept the light and who pass it frequently.[14]

Caroline eventually received the appointment and kept the light until 1885, three years after her marriage to Adolphe Autaya.

Josephine Freeman succeeded her father as keeper at Blackistone (Black Stone) Island Light Station(shown on the back cover), Maryland, in 1876 and tended the light until her death in 1912.[15]

Mary J. Herwerth succeeded her husband at Bluff Point Light Station on Lake Champlain, New York, in 1881. Like the husband of Emma Tabberrah, whom you meet in the next chapter, Mary's husband was a disabled Civil War veteran whom she assisted with his keeper's duties until his death. At that time the local superintendent of lights wrote the Chairman of the Light-House Board as follows:

> I have placed his widow Mrs. Mary J. Herwerth in charge of the Light House for the time being, and beg to submit her nomination as Principal Keeper of Bluff Point Light House at a compensation of $480 per annum, that being the salary heretofore paid the keeper of said Light House.
>
> Mrs. Herwerth is thirty-nine years old, a native of New York, received a common school education, and is in every way well able to perform the duties of the position. She is not a relative or private employee of mine.
>
> In making this nomination I beg to state that her husband volunteered in the early part of the [Civil] War and attained the rank of Captain and Brevet Major in the 91st New York Volunteers. He bore the reputation of being a brave officer, was twice wounded in battle and received a pension during his life for his disability.
>
> His widow is left without adequate means of support, with six children all of whom are minors. During the period of Major Herwerth's failing health and late sickness, Mrs. Herwerth attended to the running of the light . . .[16]

An 1881 letter from the Lighthouse Inspector to the Chairman of the Light-House Board also recommended her appointment:

> I am not in favor of women as light keepers, but this is a case which appeals most strongly to our humanity. I have no doubt that Mrs. Herwerth is thoroughly competent to perform all the duties of a light keeper, especially as she had already had considerable experience in them, and I would therefore respectfully recommend favorable action in her case. Her eldest daughter is a bright, intelligent girl, and can be of great assistance to her mother.[17]

The *Plattsburgh Republican* noted her appointment:

Bluff Point Light Station on Lake Champlain, New York, was kept by Mary Herwerth from 1881 to 1902. The light was deactivated in 1930. Courtesy of the National Archives, #26-LG-11-20.

The widow of the late Major Herwerth, light house keeper on Valcour Island, has recently been appointed to the same office. This is as it should be. Mrs. Herwerth was in charge of the light for a long time previous to her husband's death, and the work connected with the office will be just as faithfully done as ever, and this has for years been considered one of the best kept light houses on the lake.

Mary apparently continued her duties until 1902.[18]

At Squaw Point in Little Bay de Noc on the Upper Peninsula of Michigan, Kate Marvin tended the light from 1897 until 1904. Her husband had also been a disabled Civil War veteran, whose failing health forced him to give up his Baptist ministry. An influential friend in Washington arranged his appointment as keeper of the newly built Squaw Point Light Station, but Samuel Marvin died of pneumonia six months later. Kate, mother of 10 children, still had four at home and was very glad to receive his appointment. Although her closest neighbors lived six miles away and it was a 20-minute row across the bay to Gladstone, the nearest town, Kate was apparently not troubled by the isolation. Books, music, and an occasional trip across the bay were her entertainment.[19]

Not all women keepers were exemplary. In 1885 the Naval Secretary of the Light-House Board wrote the Secretary of the Treasury as follows:

> Mrs. Annie McGuire, Keeper of Pentwater Light Station, Michigan, has been reported . . . for drunkenness and irregular habits. The Inspector of the 11th Light House District, in his report of the investigation of these charges, dated 18 Feby. '85, recommends the removal of Mrs. McGuire, and the Board has the honor to request that the recommendation be complied with.[20]

Mrs. McGuire was dismissed on February 26.

[1] Letter from Thos. W. Gough; National Archives, Record Group 26, Entry 24, Box 176.

[2] National Archives, Record Group 26, Letterbook 18, "Light-House Board Miscellaneous Letters," Jan. 1853-June 1854.

[3] Personal communication with Point Lookout State Park, 1991.

[4] Sandra MacLean Clunies, "Recognizing Women's Efforts, 1861-1865," prepared for the 1998 Conference on Women and the Civil War, June 26-28, 1998, p. 3.

[5] Sandra MacLean Clunies has kindly shared some of her genealogical research-in-progress with us, including that regarding Betsy Humphrey.

[6] National Archives, Record Group 26, "Registers of Lighthouse Appointments," M1373, R1.

[7] Personal correspondence with David A. Gamage of Wilton, Maine.

[8] Letter dated Oct. 24, 1872, from Inspector Mayo to Professor Joseph Henry, Chairman of the Light-House Board, from National Archives, Record Group 26, Entry 24.

[9] Letter dated Nov. 8, 1872, from Inspector Mayo to Professor Joseph Henry, from National Archives, Record Group 26, Entry 24.

[10] Information supplied by the Monhegan Historical and Cultural Museum Association.

[11] *Women of Bay County, 1809-1980* (Bay City, Michigan: The Museum of the Great Lakes, 1980).

[12] National Archives, Record Group 26, Entry 24.

[13] Letter dated December 27, 1873, from Superintendent of Lighthouses in Detroit to the Secretary of the Light-House Board; National Archives, Record Group 26, Entry 36, Box 8. Two spellings are used for Caroline's surname: "Litogot" and "Litigot."

[14] National Archives, Record Group 26, Letterbox 371

[15] Personal correspondence supplied by the Calvert Marine Museum.

[16] National Archives, Record Group 26, Entry 36.

[17] National Archives, Record Group 26, Entry 24.

[18] From an obituary supplied by the Clinton County Historical Association.

[19] Luther Barrett, "Successful Woman Lighthouse Keeper," Delta County Historical Society Newsletter (n.d.).

[20] National Archives, Record Group 26, Entry 82.

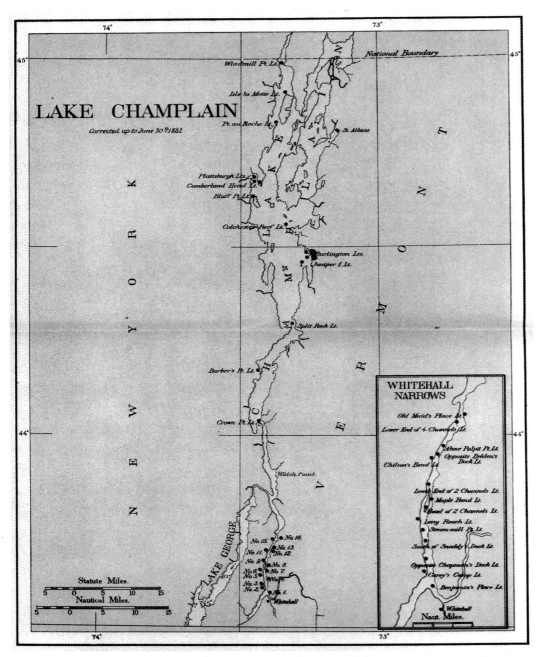

Lake Champlain Light-House map from 1881 Annual Report of the Light-House Board.

XXIII. EMMA TABBERRAH AT CUMBERLAND HEAD LIGHT STATION, NEW YORK, 1904-1919

In 1867 Emma Dominy of Beekmantown, New York, married William Tabberrah from a farm near Beekmantown.[1] Because William was a disabled veteran of the Civil War, he was advised to apply for the position of keeper of the light at Cumberland Head on Lake Champlain. He received that appointment in 1871, moving Emma and her two babies into the new limestone block quarters beside the much older conical tower.

In spite of his disability, William kept the light for 33 years. He purchased an 89-acre farm adjoining the lighthouse property, which enabled him to indulge his love of horses. The town of Plattsburgh was seven miles away, requiring horse-and-buggy transportation to reach it.

Six more Tabberrah children were born in the lighthouse. William was continually plagued by a lead bullet lodged in his hip since the Civil War. In 1903, surgery to remove the bullet led to an infection that killed him. Emma applied for his job and was appointed keeper in 1904 at a salary of $480 a year, serving until her retirement in 1919 (when she received a pension of $190.17 per year). Two of her daughters kept her company and assisted her with her keeper's duties.

The tower was 50 feet high, putting the focal beam from the Fresnel lens 75 feet above the lake level and making it visible for 11 miles. An oil room connected the tower to the keeper's house and served to store kerosene and lamps as well as a workbench and tools. The daily cleaning and maintenance of the lamps was done there.

The first floor of the keeper's house had a parlor, a dining-sitting room, and a pantry. The kitchen was in a one-story addition at the back of the house. Upstairs were two large and two small bedrooms, above them an unfinished attic. Wood stoves in the kitchen and the sitting room heated the house. Outbuildings included a carriage house, a stable for two horses, a woodshed, and an outhouse. In the nineteenth century the family did without plumbing, electricity, or a telephone.

Had Emma Tabberrah recorded her memories, she doubtless would have discussed cleaning and polishing the lamps in the oil room, as well as the daily routine of climbing the stairs at sunset to place the lamps in the lantern, replacing them with fresh lamps at midnight, and extinguishing them at sunrise. Then she carried them back to the oil room and polished them again. She would have climbed the stairs frequently to polish the many prisms of the fourth-order Fresnel lens that magnified the light.

But what her children remembered and passed on to their children were the charming details of family life in a rural lighthouse in the late nineteenth century. Rainwater for household washing and bathing was collected in a basement cistern and pumped by hand into the kitchen sink. The well on the property had a heavy concentration of sulphur, giving it a strong taste. Emma was the only one who liked it well enough to drink it. The others brought drinking water in pails from Lake Champlain.

Fortunately the local school was only a mile away so the children could walk, ski, or snowshoe up through the woods behind their home to the main road. As they grew older, three of the girls went to board in Plattsburgh while taking teacher training, and later taught in the area and downstate. As for playmates, there were very few neighbors except for summer residents in the cottages on Lake Champlain. The children were always overjoyed when cousins arrived to spend long summer holidays at the lighthouse.

The family provided its own entertainment. The children were encouraged to learn to identify the habits of woodland animals and birds. They often cared for injured birds. They played croquet on the lawn and tennis on their homemade court. They tended the garden and went on excursions to gather flowers and berries. In the summer

Emma Tabberrah, keeper of the Cumberland Head Light Station on Lake Champlain from 1904 to 1919, after her retirement. Courtesy of her grandson, Arthur B. Hillegas.

they could fish and sail on the lake and take picnics to the beach, and in winter they went ice-boating. The girls learned sewing and embroidery as well as cooking. The boys helped their father operate the farm.

The family had a piano and their father played the flute. Sunday afternoons were special because Emma dressed in her best gown and received callers in the parlor. Guests must be offered refreshments, and the children loved nothing better than bringing ice (cut from the lake in the winter and stored in an ice house in the woods) to pack into a hand-cranked ice cream freezer. They took turns working the crank and licking the paddles when it was done.

In 1894 an open-air chapel was constructed in the woods south of the ferry slip. Sunday services were conducted there by ministers of the area, as well as by some summer residents. The building was also used for occasional community picnics or a dramatic presentation by the young people.

In 1904 the Tabberrahs' daughter Rose married Milo Hillegas under the walnut tree on the lighthouse lawn. This happy occasion was followed only three months later by her father's death. He had been bedridden for two years, requiring Emma to be both constant nurse and keeper of the light.

After her 15 years keeping the Cumberland Head Light Station, Emma retired and spent another 14 years with her daughter Maud in Beekmantown, devoting her days to her children and grandchildren. She was buried beside her husband in Plattsburgh, New York.

In 1934 a skeleton tower was built by the lake shore to hold an automated acetylene light. Since the old lighthouse was no longer needed, it was sold to private owners, who in 1948 began restoration of the keeper's house as a private dwelling. In 1984 the Town of Plattsburgh adopted on its official seal a drawing of the old Cumberland Head Lighthouse.

⚜

[1] This chapter is based on material generously supplied by Arthur Burdette Hillegas, son of Emma Tabberrah's daughter Rose. Dr. Hillegas was born in 1907 while his grandmother was keeper at Cumberland Head Light Station.

XXIV. Fannie Salter at Turkey Point Light Station, Maryland, 1925-1947

The lighthouse at Turkey Point, Maryland, was built of dressed stone in 1833. Only 38 feet tall, its location on a bluff at the southern tip of Elk Neck is 100 feet above the bay, making the light visible for 13 miles.[1]

Turkey Point Light Station was kept by women longer than any other light on the Chesapeake Bay. Elizabeth Lusby kept the light from 1844 to 1861, when she died at age 65. Rebecca Crouch was appointed keeper after her husband died in 1873, and served until 1895. She was succeeded by her daughter, Georgianna Crouch Brumfield, who remained until 1919.

Fannie Mae Salter was the last civilian woman to keep a light along the 40,580 miles of coastline and river channels in the United States. When her keeper husband died in 1925, Mrs. Salter was told that Civil Service rules would prevent her succeeding him because of her age. She appealed to her senator, who went to the White House and asked President Coolidge to appoint her to the post. She was keeper at Turkey Point from 1925 until 1947.

Fannie Salter's logs are archived in the National Archives. Each day she recorded the weather, and, like Harriet Colfax, she occasionally added personal comments to her logs. Here are a few examples that show the routine of her daily life as she began her career as official keeper:

April 1, 1925: Northwest fresh, cloudy. Received telegram that I have been appointed as permanent keeper of this Station by Pres. Coolidge.

Went to North East [a nearby Maryland town] for supplies. Painted in lantern. Cleaned lens to-day.

April 6: Northeast fresh a.m., calm p.m. clear. Cleaned brass to-day.

April 9: Southwest moderate clear. Painted lantern floor & platform below. Unpacking furniture.

April 16: North to northeast fresh clear. Scrubbed lantern, cleaned cellar, pumped water out of boat.

April 20: Northeast fresh, cloudy clearing to west p.m. Keeper left 6:30 a.m. for Balto. on official business. Returned same day 10:15 p.m.

April 23: Southwest rain in early morning, but cleared off pretty. Recharged fire extinguisher.

April 27: South to west light fair. Put screens in windows, shellacked two floors.

April 29: Northeast fresh cloudy. Pumped water out of boat. Scrubbed lantern floor.

September 2: West to southwest light, partly cloudy. Cleaned storm panes inside and out.

Turkey Point Light Station at the head of the Chesapeake Bay. In 2000, only the tower remains. Courtesy U.S. Coast Guard Historian's Office.

Fannie Salter and her Chesapeake Bay retriever go about chores at the Turkey Point Light Station. Courtesy of the Ralph Smith Collection, The Mariners' Museum, Newport News, Virginia.

September 4: Light westerly winds partly cloudy. Had bushes cut down round the bank.

September 5: Northwest light, fair. Cleaned tower from top to bottom & bell house.

September 8: Light northwest partly cloudy. Mowed lawn.

September 9: Moderate southwest hazy. Tender Juniper *delivered medicine, wheelbarrow & parts for stove.*

September 10: Moderate to calm southwest, hazy, hot. Tender Juniper *passed this Station this p.m. after relighting aids to navigation up the Susquehanna.*

September 17: West moderate, clear cool. Finished painting exterior of bell house.

September 18: Moderately southerly winds partly cloudy. Whitewashed interior of toilet, painted the wood.

September 19: West moderate fair. Painted tower floor, handrail and ladder, scrubbed tower steps.

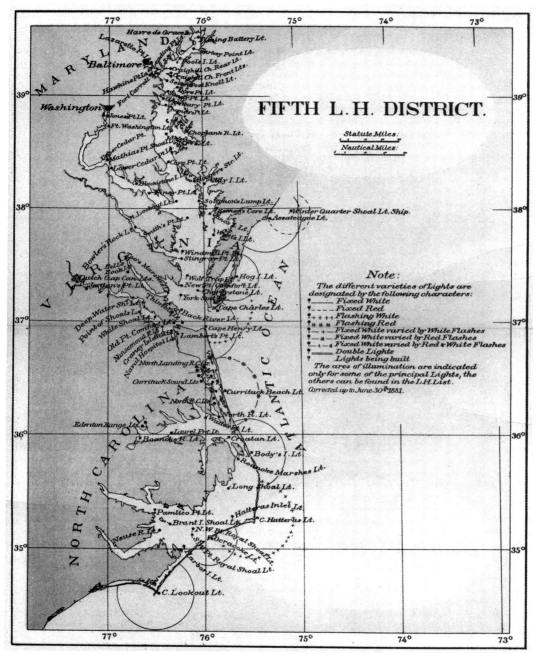

Map of Fifth Lighthouse District from 1881 Annual Report of the Light-House Board.

Fannie Salter

September 21: Tender Maple *arrived with wood & coal, also fogbell machinery, and Mr. Lenord came to install same.*

September 29: Northwest light, partly cloudy. Painted new woodwork in bell house.

Until 1943, when electricity was installed at Turkey Point, Mrs. Salter found it necessary to make four or five trips daily to the top of the tower. When a 100-watt electric bulb was placed inside the Fresnel prism, increasing the light to 680 candlepower, the keeper's time-consuming duties were reduced to the mere flip of a switch. Then one trip a day up the tower kept the light in working order. Only during cold weather were additional trips necessary to defrost the huge windows surrounding the light. The heavy brass oil lamps used earlier were kept in readiness in case the electric power and auxiliary plant should malfunction (the auxiliary plant was supposed to go into operation automatically when the electric power failed).

Like other lighthouse keepers, Mrs. Salter maintained a radio watch and was on duty seven days a week, 24 hours a day. She was in

Fannie Salter holds an electric light bulb and the incandescent oil vapor lamp which the bulb replaced. Courtesy of U.S. Coast Guard Historian's Office.

constant communication with aids to navigation authorities and made reports of local weather conditions and other necessary information by a radio telephone set, installed by the Coast Guard during World War II. Although no instruction in its use was provided, Fannie mastered the radio with the aid of the accompanying manual.

Snow-blocked roads often marooned Fannie Salter many weeks at a time during the winter, leaving radio and telephone as her only means of communication with the outside world. She fed herself from her well-stocked vegetable cellar, where shelves were lined with home-canned jars of the vegetables and fruits she grew on the lighthouse's three-acre plot. Loneliness was relieved by a Chesapeake Bay retriever, a flock of chickens, and a dozen head of lambs and sheep. In the early years of Mrs. Salter's tenure, laundry, bakery, and ice trucks made deliveries to the lighthouse, but World War II put an end to the long trips over the seven-mile road through Elk Neck State Park.

"And when I get tired of things outdoors, I always have my hobby—crossword puzzles," Fannie Salter said in 1945. "I never seem

Fannie Salter's daughter Mabel rings the fog bell at Turkey Point Light Station in the 1930s. Courtesy of the Ralph Smith Collection, The Mariners' Museum, Newport News, Virginia.

Fannie Salter polishes the Fresnel lens in the lantern of Turkey Point Light. Courtesy of the U.S. Coast Guard Historian's Office.

to get enough of crossword puzzles," she smiled. "My friends send me many hundreds, but I'm always 'fresh out.' Most of my evenings are spent on crossword puzzles and reading."[2]

Fannie Salter had three children, all married except Bradley, the youngest, who helped her with some of the heavier chores about the light station.

Talking over her early days as keeper of the light at Turkey Point, Mrs. Salter recalled one of her most frightening experiences. "It was a cold night and very foggy out," she said. "I was alone with my seven-year-old son at the time. Suddenly the whistle of a boat, apparently making for Philadelphia, was heard around our point. I started the bell ringing, but almost immediately a cable connected to the striking mechanism snapped.

"I began to pull the bell, counting to fifteen between each pull. It was necessary to ring the bell four times a minute. I kept this up for about 55 minutes, until the ship was safely around the point and headed for the Chesapeake and Delaware Canal. I was never more exhausted in my whole life. It certainly was one experience I never want to relive," she said.

Modern floating aids to navigation made the bell no longer necessary, but Fannie Salter's duties included checking and reporting on the various buoys, channel lights, and other aids in her area so they were kept in proper position and working order.

When asked about retirement plans in 1945, she said, "I plan to stay as long as the Coast Guard wants me. Perhaps after the war I'll make other plans." She smiled when she added, "Maybe I couldn't sleep away from the light. You see, its bright beam has been shining through my bedroom window for so many years its presence has become my security and companion. Whenever the light goes out I wake up immediately."

When she finally retired in 1947, she moved to a house six miles away, where she could still see her beloved light flashing. Later she lived in Baltimore until her death in 1966 at age 83.

At Turkey Point, the Coast Guard tore down the outbuildings and the keeper's house, also destroying the brick stairway in the tower so that vandals could not reach the light. The light was deactivated in 2000; a local preservation group has plans to take over the station and rebuild the keepers quarters.

⤛⤜

[1] Much of this chapter is based on a Coast Guard press release about Fannie Salter issued in 1945, written by W. W. Wilson, Sp.2c(PR), USCGR. Some details are taken from a letter written on April 21, 1979, by Fannie Mae Salter's daughter, Olga Crouch, to Clifford Gallant of Pacific Grove, California. This letter is now in the files of the U.S. Lighthouse Society in San Francisco. The authors have also enjoyed corresponding with Olga Crouch, who lives in North East, Maryland. Olga Salter Crouch's husband was related to Georgianna Crouch Brumfield, who kept the Turkey Point Light from 1898 until 1919.

Other articles about Fannie Salter include a piece that appeared in *The Sunday Star Pictorial Magazine,* April 20, 1947; an article entitled "Fannie Salter—America's Last Woman Lighthouse Keeper," by Robert O. Smith in *The Weather Gauge* (date unknown); and an obituary in the *Mobile Press Register,* 13 March 1966.

[2] Quotations are from a Coast Guard press release issued in 1945.

XXV. The U.S. Coast Guard Runs the Lighthouse Service

As the nineteenth century drew to a close, the lighthouse service was becoming more and more professional. Inexperienced amateurs with political clout no longer received keeper's appointments for life. Instead, young men were encouraged to join the service at the bottom rank, such as seaman on a tender, and work their way up, being promoted and transferred from post to post. In 1896 lighthouse keepers were included in the classified Civil Service and were expected to have specific qualifications.

Many of the lights were being electrified after 1900. Before electric power was available, many lenses were revolved by a large clockwork, propelled by a hand-cranked weight suspended inside the lighthouse tower. This old-fashioned technology was replaced by electric equipment, as were the kerosene and coal-burning boilers firing steam fog horns, eliminating the need for keepers on 24-hour-a-day duty. Traditional towers were often replaced with smaller skeletal structures that didn't require the constant attention of a live-in keeper.

In 1910 Congress replaced the U.S. Light-House Board with the U.S. Bureau of Lighthouses, located within the Commerce Department. By this date the United States had 11,713 aids to navigation (lighthouses, post lights, buoys, lightships, etc.) along its coasts and rivers. The man selected to head the new bureau, George R. Putnam, was determined to eliminate politics from the lighthouse service. District supervisor and inspector posts were transferred from military officers to civilians—generally career lighthouse service employees—thus forging a truly professional organization.[1]

The first experiments with automatic lights in lighthouses were made after World War I. The radiobeacon was introduced in light stations in 1921. It offered a much more sophisticated way for ships to determine location than depending on a landmark such as a lighthouse by day or a light by night. Neither is needed when ships have radar equipment that permits a navigator to "see" the shore up to 20 miles away on a screen.

The number of female lighthouse keepers decreased during the twentieth century. Based on the Appendix listing known female head keepers, the numbers per decade were as follows:

1820	1		1890	31
1830	8		1900	38
1840	20		1910	23
1850	40		1920	12
1860	42		1930	3
1870	49		1940	2
1880	40			

There are few official explanations as to why the number of female keepers decreased. A 1948 *Coast Guard Bulletin* included the following comments about women keepers, implying that modern technology had deprived them of lighthouse service careers:

> In days gone by, the duties and lives of these women keepers were often arduous in the extreme, but principally because of the great isolation of the sites on which many lighthouses were built, and the lack of modern conveniences. These women often performed acts of heroism, not unexpected where they lived so surrounded by the sea; and on numerous occasions made personal sacrifices that the signals under their charge might not fail the mariners.
>
> It was the development of steam for signals and their coal-fired boilers, and the later introduction of heavy duty internal combustion engines, which first placed the duties of keepers of lighthouses beyond the capacity of most women. Their gradual retirement from this field of employment was further hastened when intricate electrical equipment was placed at many stations, and when the duties of lighthouse keepers gradually came to require special training and when many of the newer stations were built offshore on submarine foundations. As these changes took place, those women who remained in the lighthouse service were

Fog signal equipment used at New Dungeness Light Station in 1908. Courtesy of the National Archives, #26-LG-62-14.

transferred to or were retained at stations where the equipment was of a more simple type. Soon still other developments and inventions were to invade the field of the woman keeper, for in those quiet backwaters, where comparatively primitive equipment was still found adequate, it was found that automatic apparatus could be effectively substituted, and many smaller lighthouses were converted into automatically operated stations or made parts of groups of lights tended by keepers who maintained a patrol by means of smaller boats. These changes practically closed the lighthouse field to women.

The 1939 list of employees in the lighthouse service indicates that a number of women were serving as lamplighters, primarily on the nation's western rivers. The 1927 *Regulations for the Lighthouse Service* defines the various posts as follows:

> When the care of a light station requires continuous watching, the employee shall be designated "keeper" and shall be given formal appointment by the department.

The designation of "light attendant" shall be used for employees in charge of minor lights requiring their full-time personal services, but not continuous watching. The designation "lamplighter" shall be used for employees in charge of minor lights not requiring their full time. No formal appointments by the department shall be given light attendants or lamplighters, but these shall be employed as provided in the Civil Service Regulations for the Lighthouse Service.[2]

Salaries for lamplighters were quite different from those of light attendants. Grace Anderson, lamplighter on the Siuslaw River in Oregon, received $300 annually, whereas Chester Anderson, a light attendant at Coos Bay, Oregon, received $2,160. Female clerks in the various district offices were paid much more than these minor attendants.[3]

The maintenance of aids to navigation was integrated into the U.S. Coast Guard mission in 1939. As part of the transition, personnel in the lighthouse service were given the choice of continuing their civilian status or converting to a military rank at no loss of pay. Those who chose to remain civilians gradually reached retirement age, and the era of the civilian keeper ended.

The Coast Guard continued the steady improvements in aids to navigation, including the introduction of loran (long-range navigation) and shoran (short-range navigation) by which the navigator determines his ship's position from radio signals received from Coast Guard stations. Coast Guard personnel (both men and women) are systematically trained to perform a vast array of duties and are periodically rotated from assignment to assignment. Today, with the exception of the light in Boston Harbor (which by special act of Congress in 1989 is to remain permanently manned to preserve its special historic character), the era of manned light stations is over. Now that larger vessels usually have more sophisticated navigational equipment such as GPS, radar, and electronic gear that can determine location via satellite, it is the smaller vessels without this equipment that rely on lighthouses for navigation. Coast Guard maintenance of active aids to navigation is now performed by small aids-to-navigation teams (ANT) who make periodic visits to check and maintain light stations. Today fewer than 400 historic light stations continue to support automated lights maintained by the Coast Guard.

Some lighthouses still use Fresnel lenses and an electric light bulb, all automated, but more powerful aerobeacons with a 1,000-watt lamp are used where needed. Some lights today consist of a simple plastic lens around a solar-powered lamp, mounted on a platform or pole— a startling contrast to the tall towers that housed the beacons in decades past. Many traditional towers support modern lenses powered by solar panels, eliminating the need for electricity in offshore locations.

Women in the Coast Guard continued to tend the lights. The light at the Dofflemyer Point Light Station near Olympia, Washington, was automated (turned on and off by a photoelectric cell) in the 1960s, but not the fog signal. In 1965 Madeline Campbell was appointed keeper of the Dofflemyer Point Lighthouse. Her husband and son helped her maintain the equipment. So important was the fog signal that they would check the weather predictions and get a sitter to operate it if they were to be away from home in foggy weather. Mrs. Campbell kept her post until the fog signal was automated in 1987. Even then, because she lived nearby she kept an eye on the station and informed the Coast Guard if anything needed attention.

In 1980, Jeni Burr, Seaman First Class, was appointed keeper at New Dungeness Light Station, located on a seven-mile-long sand spit in the Strait of Juan de Fuca in Washington State. The light had been automated in 1976, but Jeni and her husband, Eric, maintained the grounds and buildings, living in the keeper's house (built in 1905) with their five cats and two dogs. At high tide they were cut off from the mainland, so they resorted to travel by boat or timed their jeep trips to town by the tides.[4]

In the Winter 1986 issue of *The Keeper's Log*, Karen McLean was listed as keeper of three lights—the Doubling Point range lights and Squirrel Point—along the Kennebec River in Maine. Her husband Don was in charge of a nearby unit in Boothbay. They lived in a small white frame house between the two stations.

<hr/>

[1] A detailed description of the evolution of the lighthouse service can be found in Francis Ross Holland, Jr., *America's Lighthouses*.

[2] *Regulations for the Lighthouse Service* (Washington, D.C.: Government Printing Office, 1927), p. 178.

[3] "List of Lighthouse Personnel Transferred from the Commerce Department to the Treasury Department Pursuant to Reorganization Plan II of May 9, 1939," dated July 22, 1939, found in National Archives, Record Group 26, Entry 110, "Classifications of Light-House Personnel, 1925-1939."

[4] The careers in the Coast Guard of both women keepers of Washington lighthouses are outlined in Sharlene and Ted Nelson, *Umbrella Guide to Washington Lighthouses*.

EPILOGUE

Although the era of the resident lighthouse keeper has ended, our attachment to lighthouses continues. Landmarks are important to orienting us in our terrain, and lighthouse towers serve as daymarks for those on land and water alike, helping to define our sense of place. The destruction of a lighthouse tower leaves a landscape blighted, disturbingly emptied. The symbolism of lighthouses still grips us— their assurance of security for those in peril on the sea, of a lifeline to safety, of guidance to solid footing on shore.

Much individual effort is devoted to maintaining these reminders of a more romantic past. The Coast Guard tries to find custodians who will preserve the integrity of both automated stations and stations no longer needed as active aids to navigation. Imaginative adaptive uses range from marine research laboratories to bed-and-breakfast inns. Numerous historical societies and local authorities have assumed responsibility for preserving, interpreting, and keeping the lighthouses in their communities intact, often turning them into museums or historic sites that permit hundreds of visitors to explore them. At the turn of this new century there are approximately 600 surviving historic light stations in the United States, each of which once had a resident keeper. Of these, 250 are currently accessible to the public, including 35 in national parks.[1]

Although in many cases only the grounds of the stations are open to the public, visitors can still climb a number of towers and see the old Fresnel lens displayed, can create mental images of a sturdy keeper going about his duties there. If those images summon up stalwart men lighting and watching the lights night after night, regardless of monotony or inclement weather, these chapters should serve as a reminder that dozens of intrepid women also climbed those stairs and lit those lamps and polished those lenses. Their dedication to ensuring the safety of the seamen on the ships that plied our coasts and waterways matched that of their male colleagues, and they too should be remembered and honored for their courage and devotion.

❧⁂❧

[1] *Inventory of Historic Light Stations*, National Park Service National Maritime Initiative, Washington, D.C., 2000. For access to the light station inventory and other lighthouse information, visit the Lighthouse Heritage web site at <http://www.cr.nps.gov/maritime/lt_index.htm>.

APPENDIX: WOMEN WHO KEPT THE LIGHTS, 1776-1947

This appendix was initially based on the handwritten "Lighthouse Keepers and Assistants" Volume I, 1828-1857; Volume II, 1851-1871; Volume III, 1853-1871, Districts 1-8; Volume IV, 1869-1880; Volume V, 1872-1880; Volume VI, 1879-1905, Districts 6-13; and Volume VII (no dates), located in National Archives Record Group 26, Entry 92. Some of the handwriting in these registers was very difficult to read; for example, Ellis was read as Ellie, but corrected through correspondence. Nor could first names like Darrell be easily identified as masculine or feminine.

This appendix does not include dozens of women who served for a period of months (less than a year) after a father's or husband's death, while they waited for the arrival of a new keeper. Nor does it include the many women who served as assistant keepers, of whom over 240 names were tallied from the registers listed above. Several of the women whose careers are detailed in this book, however, served as both assistant keepers and keepers. Two in particular—Catherine Moore and Ida Lewis—began keeping the lights while still in their teens and spent most of their lives in lighthouses. Because their experiences as assistants have been recorded, those years are included in their chapters.

The total number of women serving as principle keepers for more than a year and included in this appendix is 140; some have been added for the period both before and after the volumes listed above were recorded and were found in subsequent research; however, we do not include women who were assigned keeper duties after lighthouses were transferred to the U.S. Coast Guard in 1939. Also in the second edition, we have not included women for whose appointments we could not find ending dates. We assume that these women served less than a year, for they did not show up in subsequent lists.

Additional research conducted for the second edition uncovered new information in the *Register of Officers and Agents in the Service of the*

United States (Washington, D.C.: 1831-1885, published in odd years only) as well as in the following entries in National Archives Record Group 26: Entry 19, "Letters Sent by the Secretary of the Treasury, April 1851-1878," Volumes 1-11; Entry 99, "Lighthouse Appointments," Vol. 1 (1849-1853), Vol. 4 (1861-1864), Vol. 5 (1864-1866), Vol. 6 (1867-1873); Entry 97, "Lighthouse Appointments, 1874-1903" (Volumes 1-4); Entry 101, "Records of Salaries of Light-House Keepers, 1849, 1881-1912" (Volumes 1, 20-25); Entry 106, "Record of the Appointment of Light-House Keepers, 1817-1903" (Volumes 1-8); Entry 16, "Miscellaneous Records, 1816-1929, 1918-1936" (Box 4: "Lists of Lighthouse Service Personnel for 1911"); and Entry 50, "Department of Commerce Correspondence 1910-1939." As there are still many question marks in this list and as we could never locate or review all available records, we welcome any new documentation our readers might provide on these and other female lighthouse keepers.

Alabama

Choctaw Point Light Station, Mobile Bay

(Mrs.) Carmalite Philibert, 1842 - 1852
Replaced: husband

California

Angel Island Light Station, San Francisco Bay

(Mrs.) Juliet Nichols, 1902 - 1914
Replaced: John Ross, deceased

Humboldt Bay Light Station, Humboldt Bay Entrance

(Mrs.) Sarah E. Johnson, 1859 - 1863
Replaced: J. Johnson (husband), deceased

Mare Island Light Station, San Pablo Bay

(Mrs.) Theresa C. Watson, 1873 - 1881
Replaced:

(Mrs.) Kate C. McDougal, 1881 - 1916
Replaced: Mrs. Theresa C. Watson, resigned

Point Fermin Light Station, San Pedro Harbor

Mary L. Smith, 1874[1] - 1882
Replaced: (new appointment)

Thelma Austin, 1925 - 1941
Replaced: father

Point Pinos Light Station, Monterey Bay

(Mrs.) Charlotte A. Layton, 1855 - 1860
Replaced: Charles Layton (husband), deceased

(Mrs.) Emily A. Fish, 1893 -1914
Replaced: Alan L. Luce, resigned

Santa Barbara Light Station, Santa Barbara Channel

(Mrs.) Julia F. Williams, 1865 - 1905
Replaced: Albert Williams (husband), resigned

(Mrs.) Caroline Morse, 1905 - 1911
Replaced: Julia Williams, resigned

Santa Cruz Light Station, North End Monterey Bay

(Miss) Laura J. Hecox, 1883 - 1917
Replaced: Adna A. Hecox (father), deceased

Connecticut

Black Rock (Harbor) Light Station, Fayerweather Island, Long Island Sound

Catherine A. Moore, 1871 - 1878
Replaced: Stephen Moore (father), deceased

Bridgeport Breakwater Light Station, West Side of Harbor Entrance

(Mrs.) Flora McNeil, 1904 - 1920
Replaced: Stephen McNeil (husband)

Lynde Point (Saybrook) Light Station, Connecticut River/Long Island Sound

(Mrs.) Catharine F. Whittlesey, 1842 - 1852
Replaced: Daniel Whittlesey (husband), deceased

Morgan's Point Light Station, Mystic River Mouth/Long Island Sound

(Mrs.) Eliza A. Daboll, 1838 - 1854
Replaced: husband

Mrs. Francis McDonald, 1869 - 1871
Replaced: A. McDonald, resigned

Stonington (Harbor) Light Station, East Side of Harbor

(Mrs.) Patty Potter, 1842 - 1854
Replaced: husband

Stratford Point Light Station, Stratford River Entrance/Long Island Sound

Amy Buddington, 1848 - 1859 or 1860
Replaced:

Delaware

Bombay Hook Light Station, Delaware River at Smyrna River Mouth

Margaret Stuart, 1850 - 1862
Replaced: Duncan Stuart (father), resigned

Mahon's Ditch Light Station, South Side Delaware Bay

(Mrs.) Susan Harvey, 1848 - 1853
Replaced: Thomas E. Harvey (husband)

Florida

Key West Light Station, Whiteheads Point

(Mrs.) Barbara Mabrity, 1832 - 1862
Replaced: Michael Mabrity (husband), deceased

(Mrs.) Mary E. Bethel, 1908 - 1913
Replaced: William Bethel (husband), resigned

Pensacola Light Station, Pensacola Bay

(Mrs.) Michaela Ingraham, 1840 - 1855
Replaced: Jeremiah Ingraham (husband), deceased

Sand Key Light Station, Florida Keys

(Mrs.) Rebecca Flaherty, 1830 - 1837
Replaced: John Flaherty (husband), deceased

St. Marks Light Station, Appalachee Bay/St. Marks River

(Mrs.) Ann Dudley, 1850 - 1854
Replaced: Needham Dudley (husband)

(Mrs.) Sarah J. Fine, 1904 - 1910
Replaced: Charles Fine (husband), deceased

Georgia

Oyster Beds Beacon & Cockspur Island Light Station, Savannah River Channel

(Mrs.) Mary Maher, 1853 - 1856
Replaced: Cornelius Maher (husband), deceased

Indiana

Calumet Harbor Light Station, Calumet Harbor/Lake Michigan

(Mrs.) Mary H. Ryan, 1873 - 1880
Replaced: husband, deceased

Michigan City Light Station, Lake Michigan

Harriet Towner, 1844 - 1853
Replaced:

Harriet E. Colfax, 1861 - 1904
Replaced: John M. Clarkson

Louisiana

Bayou St. John Light Station, Lake Pontchartrain East Entrance

(Mrs.) Annie Gage, 1895 - 1906
Replaced: Robert Gage (husband), deceased

Minnie E. Coteron, 1906 - after 1912
Replaced: Mrs. Annie Gage

Head of Passes Light Station, Deer Island, Mississippi River Mouth

(Mrs.) Jessie Fisher, 1864 - 1866
Replaced: James Fisher (husband), deceased

(Mrs.) Margaret "Maggie" Norvell, 1891 - 1896[2]
Replaced: Louis Norvell (husband), deceased

New Canal Light Station, Lake Pontchartrain New Canal Entrance

(Mrs.) Jane O'Driscoll, 1850 - 1853
Replaced: H. M. O'Driscoll (husband), deceased

(Mrs.) Mary F. Campbell, 1869 - 1893
Replaced: Augustus Campbell (husband), deceased

(Mrs.) Caroline Riddle, 1893 - 1924
Replaced: Mary F. Campbell, deceased

(Mrs.) Margaret R. Norvell, 1924 - 1932
Replaced: Caroline Riddle

Pass Manchac Light Station, West Shore Lake Pontchartrain

(Mrs.) Mary J. Succow, 1873 - 1909
Replaced: Anthony Succow (husband), deceased

Port Pontchartrain Light Station, Lake Pontchartrain

(Mrs.) Ellen Wilson, 1882 - 1896
Replaced: D. F. Powers (or Power), resigned

(Mrs.) Margaret R. Norvell, 1896 - 1924
Replaced: Mrs. Ellen Wilson, deceased

Mrs. W. E. Coteron,[3] 1924 - 1929
Replaced: Margaret R. Norvell

West Rigolets Light Station, Rigolets Channel/Lake Pontchartrain

(Mrs.) Anna M. Read, 1898 - after 1912
Replaced: John M. Read (husband), deceased

Maine

Deer Island Thoroughfare Light Station, Mark Island/Penobscot Bay

(Mrs.) Melissa Holden, 1874 - 1876
Replaced: Samuel E. Holden (husband), deceased

Monhegan Island Light Station, Monhegan Island

(Mrs.) Betsy Morrow Humphrey, 1862 - 1880
Replaced: Joseph B. Humphrey (husband), deceased

Pond Island Light Station, Kennebec River Entrance

(Mrs.) Harriet (or Hannah?) Gill, 1864 - 1867[4]
Replaced: Samuel Gill (husband), resigned

Maryland

Blackistone Island Light Station, St. Clements Island/Potomac River

(Mrs.) Josephine Freeman, 1876 - 1912
Replaced: Joseph L. McWilliams (father), resigned

Bodkin Island Light Station, Patapsco River Entrance/Chesapeake Bay

(Mrs.) Rosannah Thatham, 1844-1847
Replaced:

Cove Point Light Station, Patuxent River Entrance/Chesapeake Bay

(Mrs.) Sarah Thomas, 1857 - 1859
Replaced: George Thomas (husband), deceased

Fishing Battery Island Light Station, Upper Chesapeake Bay

Sarah Levy, 1853 - 1855
Replaced: John Levy, deceased

Havre de Grace (Concord Pt.) Light Station, Susquehanna River Entrance/Upper Chesapeake Bay

(Mrs.) Esther O'Neill, 1863 - 1881
Replaced: John O'Neill, deceased

North Point Light Station (two lights), Patapsco River Entrance/Chesapeake Bay

(Mrs.) Elizabeth Riley, 1834 - 1857
Replaced: David Riley (husband), deceased

(Mrs.) Henry Schmuck, 1864 - 1866
Replaced: Henry Schmuck (husband), removed

Piney Point Light Station, Potomac River

(Mrs.) Martha Nuthall, 1850 - 1861
Replaced: John W. Nuthall (husband), deceased

(Mrs.) Eliza Wilson, 1873 - 1877
Replaced: Noah Wilson (husband), deceased

(Mrs.) Helen C. Tune, 1877 - 1883
Replaced: Elizabeth Wilson, resigned

Point Lookout Light Station, Potomac River Entrance/ Chesapeake Bay

Ann Davis, 1830 - 1847
Replaced: James Davis (father?)

(Mrs.) Martha A. Edwards, 1853 - 1855
Replaced: Richard Edwards (husband)

(Miss) Pamela (or Permelia?) Edwards, 1855 - 1869
Replaced: Martha Edwards, resigned

Sandy Point Light Station, Upper Chesapeake Bay

(Mrs.) Mary E. Yewell, 1860 - 1861
Replaced: S. William Yewell (husband), deceased

Sharp's Island Light Station, Off Choptank River Entrance/ Chesapeake Bay

(Mrs.) Harriet Valliant, 1851 - 1856
Replaced: Jeremiah Valliant (husband), deceased

Turkey Point Light Station, Elk River Entrance/Chesapeake Bay

(Mrs.) Elizabeth Lusby, 1844 - 1862
Replaced: Robert Lusby (husband)

(Mrs.) Rebecca L. Crouch, 1873 - 1895
Replaced: John Crouch (husband), deceased

(Mrs.) Georgiana C. Brumfield, 1895 - 1919
Replaced: Rebecca Crouch (mother), deceased

(Mrs.) Fannie Salter, 1925 - 1947
Replaced: Clarence W. Salter (husband), deceased

Massachusetts

Chatham Light Station (twin lights), Chatham Harbor/Cape Cod

(Mrs.) Angeline M. Nickerson, 1848 - 1862
Replaced: Simeon Nickerson (husband), deceased

Marblehead Light Station, Marblehead Neck/Massachusetts Bay

Jane E. Martin, 1860 - 1863
Replaced:

Mayo's Beach Light Station, Head of Wellfleet Bay/Cape Cod

(Mrs.) Sarah Atwood, 1876 - 1891
Replaced: William Atwood (husband)

Nantucket Cliff Beacons, Nantucket Harbor/Cape Cod

(Mrs.) Mary Easton, 1852 - 1856
Replaced: Peleg Easton (husband), deceased

Ned's Point Light Station, East side Mattapoisett Harbor/ Buzzards Bay

(Mrs.) Hannah Brayley (or Braley), 1846 - 1848
Replaced: George Brayley (husband)

Palmer's Island Light Station, New Bedford Harbor/Buzzards Bay

(Mrs.) Caroline Stubbs, 1862 - 1873 or 1874
Replaced: James or Jacob Stubbs (husband), deceased

Plymouth (Gurnet Point) Light Station (twin lights), Plymouth Bay

(Mrs.) Hannah Thomas, 1776 - 1786
Replaced: John Thomas (husband)

Sandy Neck Light Station, Barnstable Harbor Entrance/Cape Cod

(Mrs.) Lucy J. Baxter, 1862 - 1867
Replaced: F. T. D. Baxter (husband), deceased

(Mrs.) Eunice Howes, 1880 - 1886
Replaced: James Howes (husband), deceased

Michigan

Beaver Island Harbor Point Light Station, North End Lake Michigan

(Mrs.) Elizabeth (Van Riper) Williams, 1872 - 1884[5]
Replaced: Clement Van Riper (husband), deceased

Eagle Harbor Range Light Station, Lake Superior

Mary A. Wheatley, 1898 - 1905
Replaced: Alexander McLean, transferred

Eagle River Light Station, Lake Superior

(Mrs.) Julia Ann Griswold, 1861- 1865
Replaced: John Griswold (husband), deceased

Gibraltar Light Station, Mouth of Detroit River

(Mrs.) Mary H. Vreeland, 1876 -1879[6]
Replaced: Michael Vreeland (husband), deceased

Granite Island Light Station, Lake Superior

Annie M. Carlson, 1903 - 1905
Replaced:

Little Traverse Light Station, Lake Michigan

(Mrs.) Elizabeth Williams, 1884 - 1913
Replaced:

Mamajuda Light Station, Grosse Ile/Detroit River

(Mrs.) Caroline Litigot (or Litogot?) Autaya, 1874 - 1885
Replaced: Barney Litigot (first husband), deceased

Manitou Island Light Station, Off Keewanau Peninsula/Lake Superior

Lydia Smith, 1855 - 1856
Replaced:

Marquette Light Station, Marquette Harbor/Lake Superior

(Mrs.) Eliza Truckey, 1862 - 1865
Replaced: Nelson Truckey (husband), resigned

Mission Point Light Station, Grand Traverse Bay

(Mrs.) Sarah E. Lane Grand, 1906 - 1908
Replaced: John Lane (husband), deceased

Muskegon Light Station, Harbor Entrance/Lake Michigan

(Mrs.) William M. Monroe, 1862 - 1871
Replaced: William Monroe (husband), deceased

Pentwater Light Station, Lake Michigan

(Mrs.) Annie McGuire, 1877 - 1885
Replaced: Francis McGuire (husband), deceased

Pointe aux Barques, Lake Huron

(Mrs.) Catharine Shook, 1849 - 1851
Replaced: husband, deceased

Presque Isle Harbor Range Light Station, Lake Huron

(Mrs.) Anna Garraty, 1903 - 1926
Replaced: Patrick Garraty (husband), deceased

Saginaw Bay (Bay City) Light Station, Mouth of Saginaw River

(Mrs.) Julia Brawn, 1873 - 1890
Replaced: Peter Brawn (husband), deceased

Sand Point (Escanaba) Light Station, L'Anse Bay/Lake Superior

(Mrs.) Mary L. Terry, 1870 - 1886
Replaced: John Terry (husband), deceased

Squaw Point Light Station, Little Bay de Noc, Northern Peninsula/Lake Michigan

(Mrs.) Kate Marvin, 1898 - 1904
Replaced: Samuel or Lemeul Marvin (husband), deceased

St. Joseph's Light Station, Lake Michigan

(Mrs.) Jane Enos, 1876 - 1881
Replaced: John Enos (husband), deceased

St. Mary's River Light Station

(Mrs.) Donald E. Harrison, 1902 - 1904
Replaced: Louis Metivier, deceased

Mississippi

Biloxi Light Station, Gulf of Mexico

Mary (or Maria) J. Reynolds, 1854 - 1866
Replaced: Marcellus Howard, resigned

(Mrs.) Maria Younghans, 1867 - 1918
Replaced: Perry Younghans (husband), deceased

Miranda Younghans, 1918 - 1929
Replaced: Maria Younghans (mother), resigned

Pass Christian Light Station, Mississippi Sound

(Miss) C. A. Hiern, 1844 - 1861
Replaced: Roger Hiern (father)

Mary (or Maria) J. Reynolds, 1873 -1874
Replaced: Lawrence Hyland, removed

(Mrs.) Sallie Dear, 1874 - 1877
Replaced: Mrs. M. J. Reynolds, removed

Alice Butterworth, 1877 - 1882
Replaced: Mrs. Sallie A. Dear, resigned

Round Island Light Station, Mississippi Sound

(Mrs.) Margaret Anderson, 1872 - 1881
Replaced: Charles Anderson (husband), deceased

Ship Island Light Station, Gulfport Channel/Mississippi Sound

(Mrs.) Mary R. Havens, 1855 - 1858
Replaced: Edward Havens (husband), deceased

New Jersey

Bergen Point Light Station, Newark Bay Entrance

(Mrs.) Hannah McDonald, 1873 - 1879
Replaced: John McDonald (husband), deceased

Passaic Light Station, Newark Bay

(Mrs.) Elizabeth McCashin, 1903 - 1914[7]
Replaced: D. McCashin (husband), deceased

New York

Bluff Point Light Station, Lake Champlain

(Mrs.) Mary J. Herwerth, 1881 - 1903
Replaced: William G. Herwerth (husband), deceased

Cow Island Light Station, Hudson River

Mrs. Thomas Hudson, 1853 - 1873
Replaced:

Cumberland Head Light Station, Lake Champlain

(Mrs.) Emma D. Tabberrah, 1904 - 1919
Replaced: William H. Tabberrah (husband), deceased

Elm Tree Light Station, Staten Island

(Mrs.) Sarah Ann Hooper, 1859 - 1867
Replaced: William Hooper (husband)

Fort Columbus Fog Bell, New York Harbor

Leslie Moore, 1873 - 1881 or 1882
Replaced: (new appointment)

New Baltimore Stake Light, Hudson River

(Mrs.) Eliza Smith, 1864 - 1870
Replaced: James Smith (husband), deceased

Old Field Point Light Station, Long Island Sound

Mrs. Edward Shoemaker, 1826 - 1827
Replaced: Edward Shoemaker (husband), deceased

(Mrs.) Elizabeth Smith, 1830 - 1856
Replaced: Walter Smith (husband)

Mary A. Foster, 1856 - 1869
Replaced: Elizabeth Smith, deceased

Robbins Reef Light Station, off Staten Island/New York Harbor

(Mrs.) Kate Walker, 1894 - 1919[8]
Replaced: John Walker (husband), deceased

Rondout Creek Light Station, Hudson River

(Mrs.) Catherine Murdock, 1857 - 1907
Replaced: George Murdock (husband), deceased

Saugerties Light Station, Hudson River

(Miss) Kate A. Crowley, 1873 - 1885
Replaced: Daniel Crowley (father?), resigned

Schodack Channel Light, Hudson River

(Mrs.) Joanna Lawton, 1860 - 1873
Replaced: Richard Lawton (husband), deceased

Stony Point Light Station, Hudson River

(Mrs.) Nancy Rose, 1857 - 1904
Replaced: Alexander Rose (husband), deceased

Melinda Rose, 1904 - 1905
Replaced: Nancy Rose (mother), resigned

Stuyvesant Light Station, Hudson River

(Mrs.) Christina Witbeck (or Whitbeck?), 1841 - 1853
Replaced: Jonas D. Witbeck (husband?)

Ann Witbeck, 1853 - 1866
Replaced: Christina Witbeck (mother?), removed

Throggs Neck Light Station, Long Island Sound

(Mrs.) Ellen Lyons (Kilmartin), 1876 - 1881
Replaced: Richard Lyons (husband), deceased

Ohio

Marblehead Light Station, Sandusky Bay Entrance/Lake Erie

(Mrs.) Rachel Wolcott, 1832 - 1834
Replaced: Benjamin Wolcott (husband), deceased

(Mrs.) Joanna H. McGee, 1896 - 1903
Replaced: George H. McGee (husband), deceased

Turtle Island Light Station, Maumee Bay Entrance

(Mrs.) Ann Edson, 1869 - 1870
Replaced: Nathan W. Edson (husband), deceased

Rhode Island

Beavertail Light Station, Narragansett Bay Entrance

(Mrs.) Demaris Weeden, 1848 - 1857
Replaced: Robert Weeden (husband)

Lime Rock Light Station, Newport Harbor

(Mrs.) Zoraida Lewis[9] 1872 - 1879
Replaced: Capt. Hosea Lewis (husband), deceased

(Mrs.) Ida Lewis (Wilson), 1879 - 1911
Replaced: Mrs. Zoraida Lewis (mother), resigned

Newport Harbor Light Station, Goat Island/Newport Harbor Entrance

(Mrs.) Mary Ann Heath, 1868 - 1873
Replaced: John Heath (husband), deceased

Watch Hill Light Station, Fishers Island Sound

(Mrs.) Sally Ann Crandall, 1879 - 1888
Replaced: Jared Crandall (husband or father), deceased

Warwick Neck Light Station, Narragansett Bay

(Mrs.) Abbey Waite, 1832 - 1838
Replaced: Daniel Waite (husband), deceased

Texas

Aransas Pass Light Station

Lydia Rogers, after 1908 - 1921
Replaced:

Point Isabel Light Station, Brazos Santiago

(Mrs.) Hannah Ham (or Harn?), 1860 - 1861
Replaced: John H. B. Ham (husband), deceased

Redfish Bar Light Station, Galveston Bay

(Mrs.) Lillie Ahern, 1889 - 1892
Replaced: David B. Ahern (husband), deceased

Vermont

Windmill Point Light Station, Lake Champlain

Clarinda Mott, 1859 - 1862
Replaced:

Virginia

Nansemond River Light Station, Nansemond River

(Mrs.) Ella Edwards, 1903 - 1906
Replaced: E. M. Edwards (husband)

Old Point Comfort Light Station, Entrance Hampton Roads Harbor

Amelia Deweese, 1857 - 1861
Replaced:

Washington

Ediz Hook Light Station, Puget Sound

Mary Smith, 1870 - 1874
Replaced: George Smith (father), resigned

(Mrs.) Laura Blach Stratton, 1874 - 1885
Replaced: Mary Smith, transferred to Point Fermin

Mukilteo Light Station, East Side Possession Sound

Mrs. Christiansen, 1925 - 1927
Replaced: husband

Wisconsin

North Point (Milwaukee) Light Station, Lake Michigan

Georgia A. Stebbins, 1881 - 1899
Replaced: D. K. Green (father), removed

Port Washington Light Station, Lake Michigan

(Mrs.) Margarethe Shomer, 1860 -1861
Replaced: Bernard Shomer (husband), deceased

Sand Island Light Station, Apostle Islands/Lake Superior

(Mrs.) Ella G. Quick, 1903 - 1906
Replaced: Emmanuel Quick (husband)

Sheboygan Light Station, Lake Michigan

(Mrs.) Eva Pape, 1869 - 1885
Replaced: L. Prazleton

Sherwood Point Light Station, Sturgeon Bay/Lake Michigan

(Mrs.) Minnie Cochems, after 1912[10] - 1928
Replaced: William Cochems (husband)

---

[1] Transferred from Ediz Hook, Washington Territory.

[2] Transfered to Port Pontchartrain in 1896 to replace Ellen Wilson.

[3] This may be Minnie Coteron who kept the Bayou St. John Light, Louisiana.

[4] Resigned in 1867 and replaced with William Gill.

[5] Transferred to Little Traverse Light Station.

[6] Office abolished May 1, 1879.

[7] Served as assistant keeper 1881-1903.

[8] According to a letter from the District Inspector Schley dated June 18, 1894, Kate Walker was employed as a Laborer and served as Acting Keeper of Robbins Reef Light Station from 1890-1894; letter found in National Archives, Record Group 26, Letterbook No. 993, page 446.

[9] Ida Lewis's mother was the official keeper, although, Ida performed the duties.

[10] Minnie Cochems was appointed assistant keeper in 1898; we do not know what year she was appointed keeper to replace her husband.

BIBLIOGRAPHY

Anderson, Hans Christian, *Keepers of the Lights* (New York: Greenberg Publisher, 1955).

Bachand, Robert C., *Northeast Lights* (Norwalk, Connecticut: Sea Sports Publications, 1989). Specific technical and historical information on a selection of lights on the northeast coast.

Beaver, Patrick, *A History of Lighthouses* (Secaucus, New Jersey: The Citadel Press, 1973). Lighthouses all over the world. Two chapters on American lighthouses.

Berkin, Carol Ruth, and Mary Beth Norton, *Women in America: A History* (Boston: Houghton Mifflin Co., 1979).

Carse, Robert, *Keepers of the Lights* (New York: Charles Scribner's Sons, 1969). One of the most readable of the many books about lighthouses.

Cipra, David, *Lighthouses, Lightships, and the Gulf of Mexico* (Alexandria, Virginia: Cypress Communications, 1997). Focuses on 80 light stations and ten lightships along the Gulf Coast.

Clark, Admont G., *Lighthouses of Cape Cod, Martha's Vineyard, Nantucket* (Hyannis, Massachusetts: Parnassus Imprints, Ind., 1992).

Clifford, J. Candace and Mary Louise, *Nineteenth-Century Lights: Historic Images of American Lighthouses* (Alexandria, Virginia: Cypress Communications, 2000). A collection of 230 images illustrating the evolution of lighthouses during the 1800s.

deGast, Robert, *The Lighthouses of the Chesapeake* (Baltimore: Johns Hopkins University Press, 1973). Historical sketches of Chesapeake lighthouses, with numerous black-and-white photos by the author.

Dean, Love, *Lighthouses of the Florida Keys* (Sarasota, Florida: Pineapple Press, 1998).

DeWire, Eleanor, *Guardians of the Lights* (Sarasota, Florida: Pineapple Press, 1995).

Gibbons, Gail, *Beacons of Light: Lighthouses* (New York: Morrow Junior Books, 1990). Basic information at an elementary school level.

Gleason, Sarah C., *Kindly Lights* (Boston: Beacon Press, 1991). A history of the lighthouses of southern New England.

Glunt, Ruth R., *Lighthouses and Legends of the Hudson* (New York: Library Research Association, 1975).

Great Lakes Lighthouse Keepers Association, *Instructions to Light-Keepers*: A photoreproduction of the 1902 edition of "Instructions to Light-Keepers and Masters of Light-House Vessels" (Allen Park, Michigan: Great Lakes Lighthouse Keepers Association, 1989).

Hamilton, Harlan, *Lights and Legends: A Historical Guide to Lighthouses of Long Island Sound, Fishers Island Sound, and Block Island Sound* (Stamford, Connecticut: Wescott Cove Publishing Company, 1987). A survey of both existing and former lighthouses of the area, with technical and historical information on each.

Holland, Francis Ross, *America's Lighthouses, An Illustrated History* (New York: Dover Publications, 1972). Probably the most comprehensive history of our nation's lighthouses.

_____, *Great American Lighthouses* (Washington, D.C.: The Preservation Press, 1989). A guidebook to American lighthouses.

Hurley, Neil E., *Keepers of Florida Lighthouses*, 1820-1939 (Alexandria, Virginia: Historic Lighthouse Publishers, 1990).

Johnson, Arnold Burges, *The Modern Light-House Service* (Washington, D.C.: Government Printing Office, 1890).

Jones, Ray, and Bruce Roberts, *Southern Lighthouses: Chesapeake Bay to the Gulf of Mexico* (Chester, Connecticut: Globe Pequot Press, 1989).

National Archives (Washington, D.C.) Record Group 26, "Records of the U.S. Coast Guard ,1785-1988," Entries 6, 17A, 17F, 17G, 17H, 17K, 24, 35, 36, 80, 82, 83, and 92.

National Maritime Initiative, "Inventory of Historic Light Stations," (Washington, D.C.: National Park Service, 1999); available at <http://www.cr.nps.gov/maritime/ltsum.htm>.

National Register of Historic Places, various nomination forms for lighthouses (Washington, D.C.: National Park Service).

Nelson, Sharlene P. and Ted W., *Umbrella Guide to Washington Lighthouses* (Friday Harbor, Washington: Umbrella Books, 1990).

Noble, Dennis, *Lighthouses and Keepers* (Annapolis, Maryland: Naval Institute Press, 1997).

Perry, Frank, *Lighthouse Point: Reflections on Monterey Bay History* (Soquel, California: GBH Publishing, 1982). Contains a chapter on Laura Hecox.

Putnam, George R., *Lighthouses and Lightships of the United States* (Boston and New York: Houghton Mifflin Company, 1933). Detailed description of the lighthouse service by an official who was commissioner of lighthouses for many years.

Reynaud, M. Léonce, *Memoir Upon the Illumination and Beaconage of the Coasts of France*, translated for the use of the Light-House Board of the United States, by Peter C. Hains, Engineer-Secretary of the Light-House Board (Washington, D.C.: GPO, 1876)

Rezmer, Joan Totten Musinski, *Women of Bay County 1809-1980* (Bay City, Michigan: The Museum of the Great Lakes, 1980).

Shanks, Ralph, *Lighthouses and Lifeboat Stations of San Francisco Bay* (San Anselmo, California: Costano Books, 1978). Contains chapters on Emily Fish at Point Pinos and Juliet Nichols at Angel Island.

_____, *Guardians of the Golden Gate* (Petaluma, California: Costano Books, 1990). Contains excellent chapters on Angel Island and Mare Island.

Small, Constance Scovill, *Lighthouse Keeper's Wife* (Orono, Maine: University of Maine Press, 1986).

Snow, Edward Rowe, *Women of the Sea* (New York: Dodd, Mead & Company, 1962).

_____, *Famous Lighthouses of America* (New York: Dodd, Mead & Company, 1955). Detailed descriptions of the construction of lighthouses, as well as the many shipwrecks associated with their locations. Contains a chapter on women who kept lights.

Stevenson, D. Alan, *The World's Lighthouses before 1820* (London: Oxford University Press, 1959). Lighthouses around the world before 1820, including a chapter on North American lighthouses before 1800.

U.S. Coast Guard Bicentennial Series, *The Coast Guard along the North Atlantic Coast* (Commandant's Bulletin, December 1988). Source of information about painting of Ida Lewis at Lime Rock Light.

U.S. Department of Transportation, *Chronology of Aids to Navigation and the Old Lighthouse Service, 1716-1939* (Washington, D.C.:

Public Affairs Division, United States Coast Guard, 1974). Many of the U.S. Coast Guard publications are available at <http://www.uscg.mil/hq/g-cp/history/collect.html>.

_____, *Historically Famous Lighthouses* (U.S. Coast Guard Public Information Division, CG-232).

_____, *Moments in History* (Washington, D.C.: U.S. Coast Guard Public Affairs Staff, 1990).

U.S. Light-House Board, *Instruction to Employees of the Lighthouse Service* (Washington, D.C.: 1881).

U.S. Light-House Establishment, *Public Documents and Extracts from Reports and Papers Relating to Light-Houses, Light-Vessels, and Illumination Apparatus, and to Beacons, Buoys, and Fog Signals, 1789-1871* (Washington, D.C.: Government Printing Office, 1871).

U.S. Lighthouse Society, *The Keeper's Log* (San Francisco, California: quarterly publication).

U.S. Treasury Department, *Annual Reports of the Light-House Board* (Washington, D.C.).

U.S. Treasury Department, *Organization and Duties of the Light-House Board; and Regulations, Instructions, Circulars, and General Orders of the Light-House Establishment of the United States* (Washington, D.C.: Government Printing Office, 1871).

Williams, Elizabeth Whitney, *A Child of the Sea: and Life among the Mormons* (St. James, Michigan: 1905 edition reprinted by Beaver Island Historical Society, 1983).

INDEX

A

Adams, Mrs. John Quincy 25
Ahern, David B. 223
Ahern, Lillie 223
aids-to-navigation teams (ANT) 204
Alaska purchase 151
Alligator Reef Light Station, Florida 31
Ambrose Channel, New York 167
Anderson, Charles 46, 220
Anderson, Chester 204
Anderson, Grace 204
Anderson, Margaret 46, 220
Anderson, Mary 46, 47
Angel Island Light and Fog Signal Station,
   California 73, 78, 80, 83, 210
Appleby, Joshua 28
Aransas Pass Light Station, Texas 222
assistant keepers. See keeper: assistant
Atwood, Sarah 217
Atwood, William 217
Austin, Thelma 147–150, 211
Autaya, Adolphe 184
automatic lights 201, 203, 205

B

Bach, Major Hartman 74
Bahama Islands 32
barge *Gilboa* 86
Barnstable Light, Massachusetts 10
Baxter, F. T. D. 217
Baxter, Lucy J. 217
Bay City Light Station, Michigan 182
Bayou St. John Light Station, Louisiana 213
Beaufort, North Carolina 73

Beaver Island Harbor Point Light Station,
   Michigan 138–143, 217
Beavertail Light Station, Rhode Island 222
Bergen Point Light Station, New Jersey 220
Bethel, Mary Eliza 29, 31–35, 212
Bethel, Merrill 31, 33
Bethel, William 31, 212
Biloxi Light Station, Mississippi 46, 62–70,
   193, 219
Blach, Laura 74, 223
Black Rock Harbor Light Station, Connecticut
   13–17, 211
Blackistone Island Light Station, Maryland
   184, 215
Bluff Point Light Station, New York
   184, 185, 220
boats. *See* keeper: boats for
Bodkin Island Light Station, Maryland 215
Bombay Hook Light Station, Delaware 42–44,
   212
Bombay Hook Wildlife Refuge 44
Boon Island Light Station, Maine 144–145
Boston Harbor Light Station, Massachusetts
   46, 204
Brawn, Julia Toby 182, 219
Brawn, Peter 182, 219
Brayley, Hannah 217
Brewerton, George 89, 93
Bridgeport Breakwater Light Station,
   Connecticut 211
brigantine *General Arnold* 8
British frigate *Niger* 7
British Royal Navy 6
Brooklyn, New York 169
Brown, Albert G. 64, 161
Brumfield, Georgianna Crouch 193, 216

Buddington, Amy 212
buoy tender, keeper-class 31, 50, 96, 175
buoy tender *Abbie Burgess* 50
buoy tender *Ida Lewis* 96
buoys 30
Burges, Nathaniel 8, 9
Burgess, Abbie 46, 49-56, 131
Burgess, Benji 45
Burr, Eric 205
Burr, Jeni 205
Butterworth, Alice 219

C

caisson-type lighthouse 167
California Gold Rush 71, 119
Calumet Harbor Entrance Light Station, Indiana 117–118, 213
Campbell, Augustus 213
Campbell, Madeline 205
Campbell, Mary F. 213
Cape Cod, Massachusetts 39
Cape Florida Light, Florida 37
Cape Mendocino Light Station, California 152
Carlson, Annie M. 218
Carnegie Hero Fund 93
Caroline Morse 211
Carquinez Strait, California 153
Carquinez Strait Lighthouse, California 160
cast iron 63
Central Hudson Steamboat Company 135
Chatham Light Station, Massachusetts 39, 216
Chesapeake Bay 193
    Map 196
Chesapeake Bay Maritime Museum, St. Michaels, Maryland 58, 81
Choctaw Point Light Station, Alabama 210
Christiansen, Mrs. 223
City of Tawas 106
Civil Service 136, 193, 201, 204
Civil War 31, 44, 64, 130, 151, 180, 184, 186, 189
Clarkson, John M. 213
Clunies, Sandra MacLean 30, 31, 148, 180
Cochems, Minnie 224

Cochems, William 224
Cockspur Island Light Station, Georgia 213
Coffee, Kate. *See* McDougal, Kate
Coit, Abigail 115
Colfax, Harriet 46, 93, 100, 102–117, 128, 193, 213
Colfax, Schuyler 93, 104
Commerce Department 201
Commissioner of the Revenue 20
conchology 161
Concord Point Light Station, Maryland 130, 215
Confederate Light-House Establishment 65
Congress 9, 60, 201
Connecticut Aquaculture School 17
Coolidge, President 193
Coos Bay, Oregon 204
Corwin, Thomas 128
Coteron, Minnie E. 213
Coteron, Mrs. W. E. 214
Cove Point Light Station, Maryland 215
Cow Island Light Station, New York 220
Coxe, Tench 1
Crandall, Jared 222
Crandall, Sally Ann 222
Crouch, John 216
Crouch, Rebecca 193, 216
Crowley, Daniel 221
Crowley, Kate A. 221
Cumberland Head Light Station, New York 189–192, 220
customs collector 2, 20, 37, 40, 73, 177. *See also* superintendents of lighthouses

D

Daboll, Captain 38
Daboll, Eliza 38, 211
Davis, Ann 36, 38, 216
Davis, James 36, 38, 216
daymarks 60, 168
Dear, Sallie 219
Deer Island Thoroughfare Light Station, Maine 46, 214

Delaware Bay 39
  Map 45
Delaware River, Delaware 43
Deweese, Amelia 223
Dewey, George 130, 153
district engineer. *See* engineer
district inspector. *See* inspector
District lighthouse maps 4, 19, 34, 45, 53,
  66, 72, 112, 146, 188
districts 60
Dofflemyer Point Light Station, Washington 205
Dominy, Emma. *See* Tabberrah, Emma
Dorchester Heights fortification 5
Doubling Point Range Light Station, Maine 205
Dry Tortugas Light, Florida 24, 25, 31
Dudley, Ann 212
Dudley, Needham 212
Duxbury, Massachusetts 7

E

Eagle Harbor Range Light Station, Michigan
  217
Eagle River Light Station, Michigan 217
earthquake of 1906 78
earthquake of 1925 122
Easton, Mary 217
Easton, Peleg 217
Eaton Neck Light, New York 15
Ebart, Julia 115
Ediz Hook Light Station, Washington 74, 147–
  150, 223
Edson, Ann 222
Edson, Nathan W. 222
Edwards, E. M. 223
Edwards, Ella 223
Edwards, Martha 180, 216
Edwards, Pamela 180, 216
Edwards, Richard 180, 216
electrification. *See* illumination: electricity
elevated walkway 104, 106-108
Elizabeth Van Riper. *See* Williams, Elizabeth
  Whitney
Elk Neck, Maryland 193
Elk Neck State Park 198

Elm Tree Light Station, New York 220
engineer 60, 61, 83, 98, 99
Enos, Jane 219
Enos, John 219
Escanaba Iron Port 125
Escanaba, Michigan 124

F

Fayerweather Island, Connecticut 13
Fewell, J. 65
Fifth Auditor. *See* Pleasonton, Stephen
Fine, Charles 101, 212
Fine, Sarah 100, 101, 212
Fish, Emily 73, 75, 78, 79, 83, 211
Fish, Melancthon 75, 83
Fisher, James 213
Fisher, Jessie 213
Fishing Battery Island Light Station, Maryland
  215
Flaherty, John 25, 26, 212
Flaherty, Rebecca 24–28, 212
Florida Keys
  Map 34
fog signal 71, 115, 160, 169, 180, 203, 205
  bell 78, 80, 81, 133, 143, 154, 174,
    178, 199
  horn 174
  mechanical 81, 82, 134, 199
  steam 49, 201, 202
Fogarty, Timothy 114
Fort Adams, Rhode Island 94
Fort Columbus Fog Bell 220
Foster, Mary A. 38, 221
Francis McDonald 211
Francis, Phil 162
Franklin, Benjamin 46
Freeman, Josephine 184, 215
Fresnel lens. *See* lens

G

Gage, Annie 213
Gage, Robert 213
Garden Key, Florida 24

Garfield, President 111
Garraty, Anna 218
Garraty, Patrick 218
Gibraltar Light Station, Michigan 218
Gill, Harriet 214
Gill, Samuel 214
Grand, Sarah E. Lane 218
Granite Island Light Station, Michigan 218
Grant, Abbie Burgess. *See* Burgess, Abbie
Grant, Isaac H. 49
Grant, Ulysses S. 38, 93, 111
Great Lakes 60, 103
    Map 112
Green, D. K. 223
Griswold, John 217
Griswold, Julia Ann 217
Groton, Connecticut 39
Gulf of Mexico 60, 62
    Map 34, 66
Gurnet Point Light Station, Massachusetts 1, 5–
    11, 217

H

Hackley, William Randolph 27
Ham, Hannah 223
Ham, John H. B. 223
Hamilton, Alexander 1, 9
Harris, George 74
Harrison, Mrs. Donald E. 219
Hartwell, Ann C. 104
Harvey, Susan 39, 212
Harvey, Thomas E. 39, 212
Havens, Edward 220
Havens, Mary R. 220
Havre de Grace, Maryland 130
Head of Passes Light Station, Louisiana
    177, 213
Heath, John 222
Heath, Mary Ann 222
Hecox, Adna 161, 211
Hecox, Laura 161–164, 211
Hecox Museum 164
Herald, James 148
Herwerth, Mary J. 184, 185, 220

Herwerth, William G. 220
Hiern, Miss C. A. 219
Hiern, Roger 219
Hillegas, Milo 192
Hobbs, Annie Bell 144–145
Holden, Melissa 46, 214
Holden, Samuel 47, 214
Holley, Edna 70
Hooper, Sarah Ann 220
Hooper Strait Light Station, Maryland 58, 81
Hooper, William 220
Howard, Marcellus 219
Howes, Eunice 217
Howes, George 182
Howes, James 217
Hudson, Mrs. Thomas 220
Hudson River Maritime Museum, New York 87
Hudson River, New York 84, 132, 133
    Map 19
Humboldt Bay Light Station, California 210
Humphrey, Betsy 180, 181, 214
Humphrey, Fred 182
Humphrey, Joseph B. 214
hurricanes 29, 31, 46, 69, 70. *See also* storms
    and gales

I

Ida Lewis 209
Ida Lewis Rock Light Station. *See also* Lime Rock
    Light Station, Rhode Island
Ida Lewis Yacht Club 96
illumination 12, 58, 60. *See also* lens
    acetylene 192
    Argand lamps 12, 20, 43, 46
    bucket lamps 6
    candles 6
    electricity 147, 148, 174, 198, 201, 202
    flat-wick lamps 6, 12
    Franklin lamps 68
    hydraulic lamp 31
    incandescent oil vapor lamp 174, 197
    kerosene 103, 114, 121, 147, 162,
        174, 201
    lard oil 31, 49, 68, 103, 105, 114, 121,

lard oil 31, 49, 68, 103, 105, 114, 121, 139, 147, 162
spider lamp 12
whale oil 6, 29, 46, 103
Indian Key, Florida 31
Indian wars 29
Ingraham, Jeremiah 37, 212
Ingraham, Michaela 37, 212
inspector 3, 38, 43, 60, 61, 75, 98, 99, 105, 107, 108, 111, 114, 130, 134, 151, 201
instructions to keepers. *See* keeper: Instructions

J

Jamestown 151
Johnson, J. 210
Johnson, Sarah E. 210

K

keeper
  appointments 2, 20, 25, 32, 37–39, 60, 61, 64, 128, 153, 161, 169, 177, 184, 189, 201, 209–224
  assistant 1, 20, 29, 30, 31, 32, 37, 49, 108, 114, 115, 130, 148, 168, 181, 209
  boats for 27, 46, 45, 93, 144, 174
  care of light 13, 20, 22, 31, 40, 46, 49, 74, 90, 107, 110, 122, 128, 134, 135, 139, 145, 158, 170, 189, 190, 198
  conversion to military status 204
  dangerous occupation 46–47
  domestic activities 15, 98, 110, 120, 154, 158, 160, 190, 193, 198
  education of family 17, 90, 98, 144, 154, 171, 190
  extracurricular activities (business or pleasure) 16, 29, 46, 60, 75, 119, 121, 128, 169, 186, 189, 190, 198
  instructions 20–23, 83, 98, 99, 114, 115, 128, 129, 136, 164

logbooks or journals 61, 75, 83, 98–101, 104, 114, 117, 118, 134, 193
  medical care for 61, 158
  nomination form 32
  number of female 202
  pets and domestic animals 17, 47, 75, 93, 98, 135, 178, 190, 198, 205
  record keeping 20, 22, 61, 98, 99, 109, 115, 158
  religious worship 98, 158, 192
  salaries 2, 38, 40, 110, 114, 180, 189, 204
  supplies for 21, 22, 27, 46, 48, 98, 110, 114, 120, 134, 152, 153, 169
  uniform 114
keeper's dwelling, description of 30, 43, 44, 75, 86, 89, 115, 164, 167, 190
Kennebec River, Maine 205
Key West, Florida 26, 29, 37
Key West Light Station, Florida 26, 29–35, 46, 212
Kingston, Massachusetts 5, 7
Kittery, Maine 144

L

Lake Champlain 184, 185, 188–190
  Map 188
Lake Huron
  Map 112
Lake Michigan 103, 117, 125, 138, 139, 142
  Map 112
Lake Pontchartrain, Louisiana 176
Lake Superior
  Map 112
lampist or machinist 98, 99, 110
lamplighters 203
lamps. *See* illumination
Lane, John 218
lanterns 10
lard oil. *See* illumination: lard oil
Lawton, Joanna 221
Lawton, Richard 221
Layton, Charles 73, 211
Layton, Charlotte 73, 75, 211

lens
  adoption of Fresnel lens 58
  care of 162, 198. *See also* keeper: care of light
  description of operation 48, 58, 59, 74,
    78, 162, 167, 170, 189, 201, 205
  orders 58
Levy, John 215
Levy, Sarah 215
Lewis, Hatty 93
Lewis, Hosea 89, 222
Lewis, I.W.P. 20
Lewis, Ida 46, 88–97, 222
Lewis, Rudolph 92
Lewis, Winslow 20
Lewis, Zoraida 222
Life Saving Benevolent Association of New York
    92
lifesaving 15, 21, 46, 69, 86, 90, 92, 94,
    140, 169, 178
lifesaving medal 94
light attendant 204
Light List 60, 168
light station, description of
    45, 69, 121, 144, 147, 168
lighthouse establishment, creation of 9
lighthouse tenders 46, 75, 105, 110, 134,
    152, 169, 170, 195
Lime Rock Light Station, Rhode Island 46, 88–
    97, 222
Lincoln, Benjamin 9
Litigot, Barney 218
Litigot, Caroline 182, 218
Little Bay de Noc, Michigan 185
Little Traverse Bay, Michigan 142
Little Traverse Light Station, Michigan 139–
    143, 218
logbook. *See* keeper: logbooks or journals
Long Island, New York 37
Long Island Sound 13
  Map 19
loran (long-range navigation) 204
Luce, Alan L. 211
Lusby, Elizabeth 193, 216
Lusby, Robert 216
Lynde Point Light Station, Connecticut 40, 211

Lyons, Ellen 221
Lyons, Richard 221

M

Mabrity, Barbara 29–35, 46, 212
Mabrity, Michael 29, 212
Mackinac Island, Michigan 139
Maher, Cornelius 46, 213
Maher, Mary 213
Mahon's Ditch Light Station, Delaware 39, 212
Mallory, Wm. G. 182
Mamajuda Light Station, Michigan 182, 218
Manitou Island Light Station, Michigan 218
maps. *See* District lighthouse maps
Marblehead Light Station, Massachusetts 216
Marblehead Light Station, Ohio 222
Mare Island Light Station, California 128, 151–
    160, 210
Mare Island Naval Shipyard, California
    152, 157, 158, 160
Mark Island, Maine 46
Marquette Light Station, Michigan 218
Martin, Jane E. 216
Marvin, Kate 185, 219
Marvin, Samuel 186, 219
Massachusetts Bay Colony 1, 5
Massachusetts Bay Council 6
Mather, Mary 46
Matinicus Island, Maine 45
Matinicus Rock Light Station, Maine 44–
    51, 131
May, Henry 64
Mayo's Beach Light Station, Massachusetts 217
McCashin, D. 220
McCashin, Elizabeth 220
McDonald, A. 211
McDonald, Hannah 220
McDonald, John 220
McDougal, Bessie 158
McDougal, Caroline 151, 154, 160
McDougal, Charles J. 151
McDougal, Douglas 151, 158
McDougal, Elizabeth 151
McDougal, Kate 128, 151–160, 210

McGee, Joanna H. 222
McGuire, Annie 186, 218
McGuire, Francis 218
McLean, Alexander 217
McLean, Don 205
McLean, Karen 205
McNeil, Flora 211
McNeil, Stephen 211
McWilliams, Joseph L. 215
Metivier, Louis 219
Michigan City East Pierhead Light Station,
    Indiana 115
Michigan City Harbor, Indiana 104
Michigan City Light Station, Indiana
    46, 93, 100, 102–116, 128, 213
Miller, William 9
Milneburg, Louisiana 178
mineral oil. *See* illumination: kerosene
Mission Point Light Station, Michigan 218
Mississippi Sound 63, 65
Monhegan Island Light Station, Maine
    180, 181, 214
Monroe, Mrs. William M. 218
Monroe, William 218
Monterey Bay, California 73, 75, 161
Moore, Catherine 13–17, 209, 211
Moore, Leslie 220
Moore, Stephen 13, 211
Morgan's Point Light Station, Connecticut
    38, 211
Mormons 139
Morse, Caroline 119, 120, 122
Mott, Clarinda 223
Mukilteo Light Station, Washington 223
Murdock, Catherine 84–87, 221
Murdock, George W. 85, 221
Murdock, James 87
Muskegon Light Station, Michigan 218

N

Nansemond River Light Station, Virginia 223
Nantucket Cliff Beacons, Massachusetts 217
Napa River, California 153, 160
National Archives, Washington, D.C. 98, 209

Navesink Light Station, New Jersey 59
navigational equipment 204
Ned's Point Light Station, Massachusetts 217
Neill, Fredrick 28
Neill, Rebecca Flaherty. *See* Flaherty, Rebecca
New Baltimore Stake Light, New York 220
New Canal Light Station, Louisiana 177–
    179, 213
New Dungeness Light Station, Washington
    203, 205
New England
    Map 4, 53
New Haven Light, Connecticut 15
New London, Connecticut 39
New York City 167, 169, 220
New York Harbor 171, 175
    Map 19
New York Upper Bay 166
Newport Harbor Light Station, Rhode Island
    222
Newport, Rhode Island 89, 94
Newport Yacht Club, Rhode Island 95
Nichols, Capt. Henry E. 78, 83
Nichols, Juliet 73, 78, 80, 83, 210
Nickerson, Angeline 39, 40, 216
Nickerson, Simeon 40, 216
North Point Light Station, Maryland
    21, 38, 215, 223
Northwest Passage Light Station, Florida 31
Norvell, Louis 178, 213
Norvell, Margaret 46, 176, 177, 179, 213,
    214
Nuthall, Martha 180, 215
Nuthall, John W. 215

O

Oakland, California 83
O'Driscoll, H. M. 213
O'Driscoll, Jane 213
Ogdensburg, New York 104
oil 20, 22, 58, 64, 98. *See also* illumination
oil houses 162
Old Field Point Light Station, New York
    37, 221

37, 221
Old Point Comfort Light Station, Virginia 223
Olympia, Washington 205
O'Neill, Esther 130, 215
O'Neill, Henry 130
O'Neill, John 130, 215
optics. *See also* illumination; lens
   modern 205
   reflector system 20, 22, 29, 43, 63, 181
Orleans Parish Levee Board 179
Oxfordshire, England 73
Oyster Beds Beacon, Georgia 46, 213

P

Pacific coast. *See* West Coast
Pacific Grove, California 74, 80, 83
Palmer's Island Light Station, Massachusetts 217
Pape, Eva 182, 224
Pape, Louis 182
Parkinson, Jacob 134
Parkinson, Robert 133
Pascagoula, Mississippi 46
Pass Christian Light Station, Mississippi
   65, 219
Pass Manchac Light Station, Louisiana 214
Passaic Light Station, New Jersey 220
passenger ship *Poughkeepsie* 135
Pearl Harbor 149
Pease, William C. 29
Pemaquid Point, Maine 50
Penobscot Bay, Maine 46, 46
Pensacola Light Station, Florida 25, 37, 212
Pentwater Light Station, Michigan 186, 218
Philibert, Carmalite 210
pier lights 104, 106–108, 115, 117
Piney Point Light Station, Maryland 180, 215
Plattsburgh, New York 190, 192
Pleasant Hill Cemetery, Oakland, California 83
Pleasonton, Stephen 2, 9, 22, 25, 27, 37,
   60, 128
Plymouth Bay, Massachusetts 7
Plymouth Harbor, Massachusetts 1, 5, 7
Plymouth Light Station. *See also* Gurnet Point
   Light Station

Plymouth, Massachusetts 7
Point Fermin Light Station, California 147–
   150, 210
Point Isabel Light Station, Texas 223
Point Lookout Light Station, Maryland
   36, 38, 180, 216
Point Pinos Light Station, California 73–75,
   79, 82, 211
Pointe aux Barques, Michigan 218
Pond Island Light Station, Maine 214
Pontchartrain Railroad 178
Port Pontchartrain Light Station, Louisiana
   46, 176–179, 214
Port Washington Light Station, Wisconsin 224
Potomac River 36, 38, 180
Potter, Patty 40, 212
Power, David F. 177, 214
Prazleton, L. 182, 224
Presque Isle Harbor Range Light Station,
   Michigan 218
Putnam, George R. 201

Q

Quick, Ella G. 224
Quick, Emmanuel 224

R

Racine, Wisconsin 114
radio watch 198
radiobeacon 201
railroad 71
Read, Anna M. 214
Read, John M. 214
Redfish Bar Light Station, Texas 223
reflecting apparatus 6. *See also* optics: reflector
   system
regulations. *See* keeper: Instructions
Reilly, Katy 115
rescues. *See* lifesaving
revenue cutters 22, 26
Revolutionary War 6, 134
Reynolds, Mary 62, 63, 65, 68, 219
Reynolds, Miranda 69

Riddle, Caroline 214
Riley, Elizabeth 38, 215
Robbins Reef Light Station, New York 46, 166–175, 221
Rockland, Maine 46
Rogers, Lydia 222
Rondout Creek Light Station, New York 84–87, 221
Rondout II Lighthouse, New York 87
Rose, Alexander 133, 135, 221
Rose, Melinda 133–137, 221
Rose, Nancy 132–137, 221
Ross, John 210
Round Island Light Station, Mississippi 46, 47, 220
rowboat *Rescue* 93
Ryan, Mary 117, 118, 213

S

Saginaw Bay (Bay City) Light Station, Michigan 219
Saginaw River, Michigan 182
Salinas, California 80
Salter, Bradley 198
Salter, Clarence W. 216
Salter, Fannie 131, 193–200, 216
Samuel Cullison 180
San Diego, California 71
San Francisco Bay, California 71, 78, 80
San Francisco, California 71, 80, 153
San Pablo Bay, California 153
San Pedro Harbor, California 147
Sand Island Light Station, Wisconsin 224
Sand Key Light Station, Florida 25–28, 212
Sand Point Light Station, Michigan 124–127, 219
Sandy Hook East Beacon, New Jersey 174
Sandy Hook Light Station, New Jersey 168
Sandy Neck Light Station, Massachusetts 217
Sandy Point Light Station, Maryland 216
Santa Barbara Light Station, California 119–123, 211
Santa Cruz Light Station, California 161–164, 211

Saugerties Light Station, New York 221
Savannah River channel, Georgia 46
Saybrook, Connecticut 40
Schmuck, H. 38
Schmuck, Henry 215
Schmuck, Mrs. Henry 215
Schodack Channel Light, New York 221
Schooner, Bernard 224
schooner *Herald* 107
Schooner, Mrs. 224
schooner *Rowens* 108
schooner *Scotland* 106
schooner *Thomas Howland* 140
Seaside Park, Bridgeport, Connecticut 13
Sharp's Island Light Station, Maryland 216
Shaw, Carrie 148
Shaw, George N. 148
Sheboygan Light Station, Wisconsin 182, 224
Sherwood Point Light Station, Wisconsin 224
Ship Island Light Station, Mississippi 220
shipwreck 46, 61, 86, 98, 106, 108, 119, 122, 135, 140, 169
Shoemaker, Edward 37, 221
Shoemaker, Mrs. Edward 37, 221
Shook, Catharine 218
shoran (short-range navigation) 204
Shubrick, William 38
Siuslaw River, Oregon 204
skeletal-type lighthouses 201
Smith, Eliza 220
Smith, Elizabeth 37, 38, 221
Smith, Ella 147
Smith, George 147, 223
Smith, James 220
Smith, John 39
Smith, Lydia 218
Smith, Mary 147–150, 210, 223
Smith, Victor 147
Smith, Walter 37, 221
Smyrna River, Delaware 43
Snow, Edward Rowe 8, 50, 174
Spanish-American War 78, 158
Spruce Head Cemetery, Maine 50
Spruce Head, Maine 49
Squaw Point Light Station, Michigan 185, 219

Squirrel Point Light Station, Maine 205
St. Joseph's Light Station, Michigan 219
St. Marks Light Station, Florida 100, 101, 212
St. Mary's River Light Station, Michigan 219
Staten Island depot 174
Staten Island, New York 167, 169, 171, 173
Statue of Liberty Light, New York 167, 174
steamboat *Clifton* 86
steamboat *Dean Richmond* 86
steamboat *Thorn* 86
steamships 71
Stebbins, Georgia A. 223
Stonington Light Station, Connecticut 40, 212
Stonington, Maine 47
Stony Point Fort 134
Stony Point Light Station, New York 132–137,
        221
Stony Point State Park 135
storms and gales 15, 46, 46, 48, 65, 71
        85, 90, 105–109, 144, 145, 174, 178
Strait of Juan de Fuca, Washington 71, 205
Stratford Point Light Station, Connecticut 212
Stratton, Thomas 74
Stuart, Duncan 43, 212
Stuart, Margaret 43, 44, 212
Stubbs, Caroline 217
Stubbs, Jacob 217
Stuyvesant Light Station, New York 221
Succow, Anthony 214
Succow, Mary J. 214
superintendents of lighthouses 1, 2, 20, 23,
        26, 201. *See also* customs collector
supplies. *See* keeper: supplies for
Suter, Charlotte 180

T

Tabberrah, Emma 184, 189–192, 220
Tabberrah, Maud 192
Tabberrah, Rose 192
Tabberrah, William 189, 220
Taylor, Zachary 40
Tchouticabouffa River 64
Tender Haze 105, 107
tenders, lighthouse. *See* lighthouse tenders

Terry, John 125, 219
Terry, Mary 124–127, 219
Thatham, Rosannah 215
The Pride of the Sea 122
Thomas, George 215
Thomas, Hannah 1, 5–11, 217
Thomas, John 1, 5, 7, 8, 9, 217
Thomas, Nathaniel 8
Thomas Point Light, Maryland 25
Thomas, Sarah 215
Throggs Neck Light Station, New York 221
Tompkinsville, Staten Island 175
Towner, Harriet C. 103, 213
Transcript 104
Treaty of Guadalupe Hidalgo 71
Truckey, Eliza 218
Truckey, Nelson 218
Tune, Helen C. 180, 215
Turkey Point Light Station, Maryland
        131, 193–200, 216
Turtle Island Light Station, Ohio 222
twin lights 6, 7, 10, 11, 45, 48

U

U.S. Army 60, 73
U.S. Bureau of Lighthouses 95, 201
U.S. Coast Guard 31, 50, 91, 95, 115,
        149, 175, 198, 200–206, 204, 209
U.S. Fish and Wildlife Service 44
U.S. Life-Saving Service 94
U.S. Light-House Board 3, 59, 98, 114,
        129, 201
    creation of 60–61
U.S. Marine Corps 160
U.S. Naval Academy 154
U.S. Navy 60, 152, 160
U.S. President 25
U.S. Treasury Department 1, 9, 60
University of California 75

V

Valcour Island Light Station. *See* Bluff Point Light Station, New York
Valliant, Harriet 216
Valliant, Jeremiah 216
Van Riper, Clement 139, 217
visitation at lighthouses 21, 70, 86, 98, 99, 107, 136, 145, 162, 164, 172
Vreeland, Mary H. 218
Vreeland, Michael 218

W

Waite, Abbey 222
Waite, Daniel 222
Walker, Jacob 170
Walker, John 168, 221
Walker, Kate 46, 166–175, 221
Walker, Mamie 171
War for Independence 1
War of 1812 130, 144
Warwick Neck Light Station, Rhode Island 222
Washington, George 9
Washington Hotel, Monterey 74
Watch Hill Light Station, Rhode Island 222
Watson, Theresa C. 210
Wayne, Mad Anthony 134
Weeden, Demaris 222
Weeden, Robert 222
West Coast 60, 71
  Map 72, 146
West Rigolets Light Station, Louisiana 214
western rivers 203

Wheatley, Mary A. 217
Whitehead Light Station, Maine 45, 49, 50, 214
Whittlesey, Catherine 40, 211
widow appointments, policy for 128, 184
Williams, Albert 211
Williams, Bion 119
Williams, Daniel 142
Williams, Elizabeth Whitney 138–143, 217, 218
Williams, Frank 121
Williams, Johnson 119
Williams, Julia 119–123, 211
Wilson, Elizabeth 180, 215
Wilson, Ellen 176, 177, 214
Wilson, Noah 215
Wilson, William 94
Windmill Point Light Station, Vermont 223
Witbeck, Ann 221
Witbeck, Christina 221
Wolcott, Benjamin 222
Wolcott, Rachel 222
World War II 149, 198
Worthylake, George 46
wreck. *See* shipwreck

Y

Yewell, Mary E. 216
Yewell, S. William 216
Younghans, Maria 46, 62–63, 69, 219
Younghans, Miranda 62–63, 68, 219
Younghans, Perry 68, 219

About the Authors

The second edition of *Women Who Kept the Lights* is the third collaboration between and Mary Louise and Candace Clifford. They published the first edition in 1993, and in January 2000 introduced *Nineteenth Century Lights: Historic Images of American Lighthouses.*

Mary Louise Clifford is the author of 15 books, including several introductory studies of Third World counties, social studies texts, and three novels. Her most recent book, *From Slavery to Freetown: Black Loyalists after the American Revolution*, traces the saga of the American slaves freed by the British during our War for Independence, who in 1792 became the founders of Freetown in West Africa.

Candace Clifford coordinates lighthouse preservation activities for the National Park Service's National Maritime Initiative Program. In addition to maintaining an inventory of light stations around the United States, she has coordinated cooperative lighthouse projects that have included the production of the *Historic Lighthouse Preservation Handbook.*

Lighthouse titles available from Cypress Communications

Women Who Kept the Lights: An Illustrated History of Female Lighthouse Keepers (**second edition**) by Mary Louise Clifford and J. Candace Clifford

> Available in softcover (ISBN 09636412-4-7); list price $22.95 and hardcover (ISBN 09636412-5-5); list price $32.95.

Nineteenth-Century Lights: Historic Images of American Lighthouses by J. Candace Clifford and Mary Louise Clifford

> In 1800 the United States had 26 lighthouses. At the end of the century that number had increased to over 650. As the country expanded, the building of new lighthouses followed the nation's shipping interests—down the Atlantic coast, up the Hudson River and along Lake Champlain, into the Chesapeake Bay, along the Gulf Coast, around the Great Lakes, and finally the entire length of the Pacific coast.
>
> As the number of lighthouses grew, the architectural styles of the stations and the technology that lit them changed. Rubblestone and wood were supplemented by cut stone and brick. Tall heavy towers, which sunk in the soft sands of the Chesapeake and Gulf Coast, gave way to lightweight offshore screwpiles supporting simple wooden dwellings with a lantern on the roof.
>
> The charm and surprising diversity of lighthouses are captured in these historic photographs, illustrating an important chapter in our rich maritime heritage. Published in 2000, *Nineteenth-Century Lights* is 295 pages and includes 230 illustrations, endnotes, bibliography, and index. It is available in softcover (ISBN 09636412-3-9) for $24.95 and hardcover (ISBN 09636412-2-0) for $34.95.

Lighthouses, Lightships, and the Gulf of Mexico by David L. Cipra

> Eighty light stations were built on the Gulf Coast between 1811 and 1939. Shifting bars and bayous, soft and muddy bottoms, coral reefs, and periodic hurricanes challenged the skills of lighthouse designers and builders, as well as of the men and women appointed to keep the lights. Ten lightships marked the navigable waters offshore until new building techniques to overcome the many hazards were successfully engineered. Author David Cipra presents an overall survey of the shaping influences and major events of Gulf Coast history (including the Civil War), as well as the specific history of each lighthouse and lightship that has served as an aid to navigation on the coast of Texas, Louisiana, Mississippi, Alabama, and Florida. *Lighthouses, Lightships, and the Gulf of Mexico*, 280 pages, is softcover (ISBN 09636412-1-2), retails for $24.95, and includes 93 historic photos and drawings, endnotes, bibliography, and index.

To order, make checks payable to "Cypress Communications" and send to 35 E. Rosemont Ave., Alexandria, VA 22301. (No shipping charges on prepaid orders.) For more information email <cypress@sitestar.net>.